MEMOIR OF A MILK CARTON KID

THE TANYA NICOLE KACH STORY

MEMOIR OF A MILK CARTON KD

TANYA NICOLE KACH
WITH LAWRENCE FISHER

TATE PUBLISHING
AND ENTERPRISES, LLC

Published by Tate Publishing & Enterprises, LLC
127 E. Trade Center Terrace | Mustang, Oklahoma 73064 USA
1.888.361.9473 | www.tatepublishing.com

Tate Publishing is committed to excellence in the publishing industry. The company reflects the philosophy established by the founders, based on Psalm 68:11,
"The Lord gave the word and great was the company of those who published it."

Book design copyright © 2011 by Tate Publishing, LLC. All rights reserved.
Cover design by Kenna Davis
Interior design by Stephanie Woloszyn

Published in the United States of America

ISBN: 978-1-61346-759-6
1. True Crime / General   2. Biography & Autobiography / General
11.08.19

ACKNOWLEDGEMENTS

With much gratitude to all those who supported me during the five-year journey toward the destination of this book, it would be impossible to name everyone who helped me along the way. From my family to my friends and colleagues, thank you for your unwavering encouragement and interest in my writing.

—*Lawrence H. Fisher*

CONTENTS

A STORY OF SURVIVAL AND FAITH
FOREWORD

BY BONNIE HEARN HILL

I met Lawrence Fisher on the telephone, and if I had to reduce my first impression of him to a single word, I would say, "passion." It was there in his rich voice, and in the words he spoke as we discussed his former client, Tanya Kach. He had decided to help Tanya write a book about her abduction and ultimate escape, he told me, despite the attention and publicity he would have rather shunned. He felt compelled to share Tanya's story. Perhaps, just as important, he and Tanya wanted to warn other women what can happen when you are too young, too angry, and too willing to trust the wrong man.

Over this and subsequent discussions, I soon learned that Lawrence Fisher, Law to most of us who know him well, is no ordinary attorney. He is a civil rights expert who writes poetry. He is a gifted man who pays as much attention to his heart as to his head. When he came into Tanya's life, she needed not only protection, but validation. He gave her both. Tanya had been held captive for ten horrifying years. Her self-esteem was nonexistent. Law was not only her attorney, but her friend. He was more than just her voice in the land of court. He also helped her to learn how to drive a car. He introduced her to his dogs. He enjoyed the Lenten fish fry at Tanya's church where they also worshiped together. Most of all, he cared about her.

The story you will read here is Tanya's, a teen whose life was stolen because nobody loved her enough to stop the tragic chain of events that took her from troubled middle school student to a pedophile's captive. Though Tanya is from southwestern Pennsylvania, I heard about her story in California from the time it was breaking news more than five years ago. The first time I read in our local newspaper about her escape, I wondered what it would take for a young woman, captive since the age of 14, to find the courage to risk leaving her prison—the bedroom of the man who'd abducted her. His parents lived below and, if we are to believe their claims, had no idea their son and grandson were not alone in that bedroom.

I'm looking at two photos of Tanya right now. One is the defiant blond-haired teen who had no idea what lay ahead. This is the photo that appeared on milk cartons across the country. The second is a more mature Tanya, beautiful and all in white as she confronts her accuser in court.

When Tanya escaped, media outlets, from Oprah to MTV Japan, came calling. Over the next five years, the media followed with rapt attention as Law commented (and advocated) on her behalf. At that time, Tanya wasn't ready to speak of her remarkable ordeal and redemption. She was healing. Now she has opened herself up in the pages that follow, and I only wish that what you are about to read was fiction. In reality, Tanya Kach lost her innocence in the worst way possible. Her courage and faith helped her find her way out of the nightmare. With Law Fisher, she is ready to share her story.

INTRODUCTION:
THE LONG HAUL

BY LAWRENCE H. FISHER

If it hadn't been for a property dispute, I probably wouldn't have met Tanya Kach. Until one day in March of 2006, my client, Jerry Kach, never mentioned the existence of a daughter, let alone that she had been missing for ten years. Our business was limited to talk about the boundaries of his land and his neighbor's encroachment on them.

Then, on March 21, the story of Tanya's rescue from the hands of a pedophile riveted the world. Reporters descended upon her father's house. His phone rang incessantly with interview requests. As the quarrel with his neighbor dissipated into a distant concern, he called me.

That day, my law office in Canonsburg, Pennsylvania—just outside of Pittsburgh, in the southwest part of the state—buzzed with gossip and theories regarding what had really happened to this girl, who had been abducted at the age of fourteen and kept by her abductor upstairs in his parents' home for more than a decade. I paid little attention and could not understand the incredible buzz that was going on.

"What do you think about Tanya Kach?" one of my paralegals asked me. "Do you suppose she's related to Jerry Kach?"

"I doubt it," I replied, for, at the time, Jerry Kach was one of seven hundred files in my head.

Moments later, he was on the phone, asking if I could help his daughter with the overwhelming media attention she was receiving. I was blown away but willing. We set up an appointment to meet a few days later.

Before I even had a chance to meet Tanya, a headline from the front page of a local newspaper caught my eye. Yet another above-the-fold story in the continuing coverage of the Tanya Kach case, it informed me that I had been named "spokesman" to the Kach family. Immediately, I phoned Jerry, and he apologized for failing to advise me of his family's hasty public declaration. When I arrived at work, the national and international media outlets were already calling. This prelude to meeting any client would have been remarkable in its own right, but in this case, it prepared me only to expect that everything to come was nothing like I had ever known in my career.

Four days after that, I sat in the Kach home and met with Tanya for the first time.

She came down the stairs wearing a white, fluffy bathrobe and smoking a cigarette. Her blond hair was styled, and she seemed both wary and distracted.

"Tanya, this is the attorney I told you about," Jerry said. "He's going to help us."

"Okay." She shook my hand. "Nice to meet you."

"What do you envision me doing for you?" I asked her.

"I don't know." She took a drag of her cigarette. "My dad brought you here."

"I think you have a lawsuit on your hands," I told her. "I see liability here, because you were abducted by a school security guard."

As she was a troubled kid at the time of her disappearance, I also told her that the police and school officials were indifferent to her plight and problems, as well as unwitting conspirators in her abduction. It was almost as if they were glad when she disappeared, as if she were a problem solved.

Finally, I handed her a contract and watched her seemingly skim over the pages.

"Five years?" she asked moments later, and I realized she had read every word of it.

"I really think it's going to take me that long to do for you what I need to do," I told her.

"Then I guess I'm in it for the long haul, huh?" And with that, she signed the contract.

At that moment, I knew for certain what I had suspected in the days leading up to my first encounter with Tanya. My life was going to change forever.

Serving as her counsel for nearly four years thereafter, I reviewed thousands of pages of documents pertaining to her life, ranging from education records to police reports to materials related to family legal issues. Through countless conversations with her, as well as scores of people associated with her story, and most of all, through our growing friendship, I became the only person other than Tanya who knew as much about her life. When my legal representation on her behalf ended in late December of 2009, it was only natural that I be the one to help her tell her story.

This is the story behind the headlines, Tanya's life before, during, and after her bizarre abduction and abuse. I hope the information revealed here causes you to question the fabric of society—including our justice system, our public schools, the police, the media, and the evils that lurk among us. Just as important, I hope it leaves you with the belief that the human spirit can prevail over the worst societal flaws. Regardless of how you perceive what you are about to read, a young girl lost her innocence. Yet the resilience and faith that she demonstrated in overcoming such adversity serve as reminders that nothing in life is more than any one person can handle. Tanya Kach is proof of that. This is her story.

"In the little world where children have their existence, whosoever brings them up, there is nothing so finely perceived, or so finely felt, as an injustice."

—*Charles Dickens*

FROM IDEAL TO ISOLATION AND ABUSE

My first memory of life is one of light. The closed door to my bedroom made me feel caged, imprisoned. I pulled myself up in my crib and cried. Then, one of my parents must have opened the door, and I glimpsed a crack of light that both fascinated and comforted me. In a way, that first memory is a metaphor for what kept me alive for the ten dark years of captivity I endured. Despite my abductor's repeated message that no one cared about me, despite the threats of what would happen if I tried to escape, that glimmer of hope within me never died. It was the divine lifeboat I clung to at my most desperate moments. *One day I will leave here*, I promised myself. *One day, I will tell my story.*

Although writing it has not been easy, doing so has shown me how easily a child can disappear and how simply a life can be erased. That's what happened to me. Because of that, I look at the many photos on milk cartons differently than others do. Those buck-tooth smiles and blurry, black-ink images are real kids, real people. I know, because I was one. More than 55,000 children younger than eighteen are abducted by nonfamily members every year, yet we seldom hear what ultimately happened to them. My image appeared on approximately four hundred million cartons during the time I was held captive, yet the very people who might have suspected where I was being held did nothing.

I was born in the rural community of Monongahela, Pennsylvania. Located only about seventeen miles from Pittsburgh in southwestern Pennsylvania, this town could not be farther from the big city. Fewer than ten thousand people reside there, and it is barely two square miles. Park Avenue, a two-mile stretch of road in Monongahela, has fostered a remarkable number of notable people, most famous among them National Football League Hall of Fame quarterback Joe Montana. I spent the first twelve years of my life there. My mom, Sherri, and father, Jerry, were high-school sweethearts, and I'm an only child. Since his graduation, my father was a union butcher and earned a decent living. My mom worked at McDonald's, and I loved visiting her there. In sixth and seventh grade, I was thrilled that my school bus stop was located right in front of the Golden Arches where she worked.

Mom and I loved to shop for clothes, makeup, and perfume, and my parents took me on many vacations to Florida. Before I turned thirteen, I had visited Disney World three times. Although I delighted in these trips, I couldn't understand why my parents were so serious. I was the only one who laughed, the only one who wasn't buried in a silence I couldn't understand.

Our family frequently watched fireworks and attended carnival festivities at Monongahela's Aquatorium, a great park where we walked the banks of the river and fed the geese and ducks. On one of our visits when I was only four, a man motioned me toward him with a stuffed yellow banana. The bright color attracted me, and no one seemed to notice the man in the shadows of the people. At that moment, my father began playing a coin-toss game. Other than telling me not to wander off, he paid no attention to me as he began tossing coins. My mom ventured over to another part of the grounds to play bingo. The draw of the yellow banana was so irresistible that I walked toward the man I did not know.

Once I was at his side, he kneeled down, handed me the yellow banana, and asked, "What is your favorite stuffed animal?"

"My kitties," I said, growing more comfortable with him.

"I have lots of kitties." He pointed to a car across the lot. "Would you like to go play with them?"

He extended his hand. I reached for it.

Just then, my father finally noticed that I was gone.

"Tanya Nicole," he shouted. "Where are you?"

His voice broke the stranger's spell. I darted away, terrified, and back to my father.

He did not notice the stuffed banana I was still carrying. Nor did he notice that I had been lured away from him. Instead, he scolded me for leaving his side.

"Don't you ever wander off again," he said. "You stay by me or your mom. Understand?"

Only later that evening, when my paternal grandmother noticed the toy and questioned me about it, did the ominous events of the day become apparent. By then, it was too late to find the man who seemed ready to prey on a four-year-old girl. I had narrowly escaped one abductor, yet ten years later, I would fall prey to another.

For most of my first decade in Monongahela, I loved Bible school and Bible camp. Through crafts and stories, I discovered the Methodist faith I cherish today. At Bible camp one summer, we were encouraged to sign a contract to remain chaste until marriage. I signed it happily and never doubted that I would save my virginity for my future husband. I was wrong.

I was also a Girl Scout, and when it came to selling cookies, I was the best. Getting people to buy those delicacies, especially my favorite, lemon wafers, was easy for me, maybe because I liked them so much. At the time, I thought I had a happy childhood. Although something was a little off at home, I was involved with being a kid—taking dance and baton lessons, singing in the choir, and learning to play a musical instrument. Sure, my parents were probably too quiet, but I didn't dwell on the dark spots in my life. I focused on the light.

Of my many friends in Monongahela, I was closest to Ricky Ashcraft, who lived with his parents, his sister, Leanne, and their Chinese War Dog, Kia. I had known Ricky long before we attended elementary and middle school together. His house was only two blocks from mine, and he had protected me from Timmy, the neighborhood bully. When not picnicking, we rode our bikes through the streets of Monongahela, often to the Aquatorium to feed the ducks. We also rode to the ancient Indian burial grounds. The rest of the time, we spent hours in each other's homes listening to music, watching television, and playing checkers or Monopoly.

When we played together at Ricky's house, however, Ricky's dog remained locked in the basement, because she could be vicious. God help the neighborhood when Kia got loose. Kids would jump up onto the hoods of cars when that happened. Still, one time, I asked to pet her, and Ricky's father held Kia so that I could. The dog was soft and beautiful.

When we were old enough to attend school, we ended up in the same grade and classroom. By the time we entered sixth grade, this close friendship had developed into my first-ever crush. In my eyes, Ricky was perfect, with his sandy-blond hair and sweet smile. His hazel eyes were the most beautiful I had ever seen. Besides, he always made me laugh. There was only one way to handle these new emotions of mine—tell Ricky.

I realize now that I was popular, outgoing, and extremely confident for my age. I had no trouble expressing my feelings to an unsuspecting Ricky.

"But you're my friend," he told me, looking puzzled and more than a little uncomfortable. "You'll always be my friend. Besides, you're really cute, Tanya. You can get any guy you want."

"You think so?"

"Sure. You're gorgeous."

So, there I was, happily back as Ricky's best friend. I didn't feel rejected, and I knew he wouldn't lie to me about anything, especially the part about getting any guy I wanted. All the way back when I was in kindergarten, coloring side-by-side with another student named Josh, he had asked if I liked his picture, and when I leaned over to look, he planted a kiss on me. Since then, other boys had expressed their interest in more subtle ways.

After Ricky pointed out what, to him, was obvious, I began to notice the attention I was receiving. I also began a diary reflecting my new boy-crazy state.

"I love Pat."
"I love Bryan."
"I love Steve."
"I love Justin"
"I love Mike."
"I love George."

A typical passage in this diary shows the kind of innocence that enveloped my life up to that point, and it also shows how early I began catching the lustful attention of boys.

> "I met a boy named Joshua. He's cute. We kiss each other's hands once in a while, and we hold hands and sit close. Right now I can't talk because I have no voice. I am sick and have a temperchor of 99°. Well Josh might come over this weekend. I hope he does. Today we separated the couch. He sat on one side, and I sat on another, but he crossed, so I picked up his hand and put it on his side. He started rubbing my pinky. So I moved. Well, gotta go bye."

My early diary entries show a tendency for summary, as each entry ends with a characterization of the day: *"Boring day, nice day, pretty nice day, pretty half & half day, bad day, stupid day, great day, good day, dumb day, ok day, cool day, okay day, rad cool day, lousy day,"* and so on.

Near the end of this diary, on May 6, 1995 (when I was thirteen), I wrote, *"Sup. I ran away tonight + George is worried sick about me. He started crying. . . I'm home now. 2 hour lecture."* Two days later, I wrote: *"Sup. George wants to do it (sex) with me. See I'm ready mentally, but not physically. Plus I'll break a promise to God."*

George Roberts was not all that cute, but I thought of him as a friend. Nevertheless, I was becoming more and more aware of my awakening femininity.

Unfortunately, a few years prior to this last diary entry, my parents began experiencing a widening strife in their marriage, which, in due course, separated me from Ricky, George, Josh, and my other friends. Aside from an affair my mom had when I was two years old, no signs of trouble in my parents' marriage surfaced until about the time I was seven. At that time, my father suffered a bad case of pneumonia that put him out of work and into a hospital for a long period. This prolonged illness caused financial hardship for our family because my mom loved to shop, and my father had no income while he remained hospitalized.

Mom ran up large debts, and the financial stress corresponded with what we would soon learn was her deteriorating mental health. Back then, I just thought of her behavior as "acting weird," like when she insisted that someone at a Laundromat was stealing her clothes. In the following years, Mom began repeating words and phrases inanely. She burst into laughter for no apparent reason. Ultimately and inexplicably, she set fire to a coffee table inside our home.

She also engaged in sex with all sorts of men for money. In time, my mom's mental illness tore me from the comfort of friendships and the life I knew in Monongahela. Before then, I endured family fights and breakdowns that challenged my belief in everything except God.

As my parents' marriage slowly crumbled, I often found myself alone at home, with only my prayers for my mom's attention. Although I begged her to spend time with me, hid her car keys and coat, and waited up until all hours of the night for her to return home, I could not stop what was happening. My father slept after long shifts at work, and my mom, when she did return home, was drunk.

In late 1994, I picked up a ringing phone and heard the voice of a man with whom I knew my mom was having an affair.

"You can't talk to her," I told him. "It's wrong."

"You little bitch," he said.

I slammed down the phone.

After that, my mom became extremely abusive. Not knowing how to respond, I retaliated by calling her a whore and a slut.

As I turned the corner into my teenage years, my diary passages describe the parallel way my life in Monongahela was falling apart in the wake of my parents' failing marriage. Instead of concluding my entries with summarizations about the day—good or bad—I scratched out entire entries. All of a sudden, Brian H. is a *"Jack ass!!"* and *"Tiffany can be such a bitch."* I started to worry about being "dead" and feared that my mom wanted to kill me.

Then came the traumatic court battles between my parents. Not only did I have to witness those battles, but I had to testify about my mom's spiraling mental state, as well as the abuses I had suffered at her hands. In an old stone courthouse, the judge and the lawyers were kind and understanding, but my testimony was driven by anger. Bitterly, I described how my mom once slammed my head into the wall and, following the bloody aftermath, choked me. I testified about the time she raged while pulling my hair and kicking my legs so hard that she left bruises. I also detailed the time that, while waving a steak knife in my face, she screamed, "I'm going to fucking kill you, bitch." Finally, I testified that I was afraid of my mom and that when I told my father about the abuse, his cold reaction was to initiate legal action. No other reaction. No comfort. No fatherly anything. All he wanted was to get rid of her.

He never told me what was going on in the legal proceedings or even attempted to explain anything about my mom's mental illness. Instead, he made sure that I dressed appropriately for the court appearances. In an armoire where he kept my "good clothes" under lock and key, he selected what I would wear for court appearances.

In court, my childhood friend, Ricky Ashcraft, testified about one incident when we were talking on the phone and my mom assaulted me. I had screamed for Ricky to call 911, but instead, he had told his parents, and they rushed over to our house.

The judge didn't seem all that interested in that story of my abuse. Instead, he asked Ricky if he were my boyfriend.

"No," Ricky said shyly. "Tanya's my best friend."

The legal warfare between my parents was more than I could handle. I wondered why God had made my life so unbearable. Ultimately, my mom was evicted from our home and briefly committed, involuntarily, to an institution for mental health treatment. Custody of me was awarded to her father several months before my thirteenth birthday. That was when my life changed for the worse.

Although my mom had been displaced by court order, this did not save me from her madness. She attempted to break into our home and tossed a brick through our front window. She even parked her car on the street outside of the house and stalked my father and me constantly. Again, my father did not help me to deal with the situation. He sent me out to the car to ask my mom to leave.

Once, I wakened in the middle of the night and saw him changing the locks on the front door. When I asked him why he was doing that, he said only, "Go back to bed."

Another time, my mom followed me back to the house and tried to force her way inside. My father called the police. In the insanity that ensued, my mom lied to a magistrate and secured a court order that briefly allowed her back that night with my father and me in Monongahela. I was so scared that, on the night when she was allowed back in our home, I called George to come and stay with me in the basement. I really was afraid that my mom was going to try to kill me. George and I stayed up all night, talking and listening to my mom's movements as the floorboards creaked and scuffed above us. My father had the order allowing her back into our home rescinded the next day. My parents were divorced soon after.

Quickly after the divorce, my father and I moved to McKeesport, Pennsylvania. He had begun dating Jo-Ann McGuire, a divorced woman who lived there. They had met through a dating service, and my father was impulsive in his need for female companionship. Since Jo-Ann had a seven-year-old son, Kevin, her experience with children appealed to him. More important, Jo-Ann wanted us to move in and was willing to watch over me.

Almost immediately after we moved in with her and her son, Jo-Ann alienated me. She planned fun activities for herself, Kevin, and my father, while excluding me. She justified these exclusions because I had started smoking. When the family was out having a good time, I was usually home alone. As further punishment, Jo-Ann unplugged the only telephone in the house and took it with her when leaving me behind. She removed my bedroom door so that I had no privacy. Unless she and my father were lecturing or punishing me, I felt completely ignored and unimportant. My father gave me no comfort at all. Totally subservient to Jo-Ann, he abdicated all responsibilities to her, and I grew to despise both Jo-Ann and my new home in McKeesport.

Although McKeesport is also located on the Monongahela River, five miles downstream from the town of Monongahela, for me, it was a world away in more ways than one. The steel mill town had struggled after the demise of the steel industry, and the depressed people who lived there reflected the mood of the town itself. During the height of the steel industry, McKeesport boasted more than fifty-five thousand residents and boomed with commerce and culture. In its best days, it was the site of the first, now defunct, G. C. Murphy 5 and 10 Cents Store. When the entire American steel industry fell apart in the world market during the 1970s, the town lost more than half of its residents, the most qualified of whom moved in search of employment. The tremendous loss of jobs rippled out into expansive business failures and abandoned buildings, as well as the loss of tax revenue and the decline of city services. The performance of McKeesport schools languished well below national standards.

After my parents' separation, I was transferred to the Cornell Intermediate School in McKeesport. From the start of eighth grade, in 1995, I was separated from my friends and the familiarity that had served me so well to that point. This upheaval in my world would have been difficult for any thirteen-year-old child, and I was especially nervous on my first day at Cornell. Although it was no larger than my previous school, I didn't know my way around the place. My homeroom teacher assigned a classmate, Monica Krimm, to show me. Unfortunately, Monica was a less-than-stellar student who bragged that she cut class and got into fights all the time.

At the end of the day, as she was leaving school, Monica asked me if I wanted to be friends.

"Yes," I said.

As days went by, Monica introduced me to other students, and I made some other new friends at Cornell. Still, the McKeesport students at this new school largely presented me with culture shock. There were black students, and I had never known anyone from that culture before. Some of the fourteen-year-old girls openly discussed sexual liaisons with older boys. I didn't know how to relate. I didn't fit in, and my interest in school waned.

All the while, I still yearned for the attention that my mom could not and my father would not provide. I began skipping classes and running away from my father and Jo-Ann to—as strange as it may seem—my mom, who could not take care of me and who had abused me in the past. It was during this time, in the autumn of 1995, that I met the Churchfield family, who lived up the street from Jo-Ann McGuire. Kevin Churchfield was one of the typically dead beat residents of the area, although he was married and had two children. He noticed me right away and asked me to babysit for his children. Almost immediately, he offered me marijuana. I didn't like it, but that didn't stop him.

He then began propositioning me for oral sex. He would ask me over and over again, "BJ when?"

On the one hand, being propositioned by a man in his forties repulsed me. On the other hand, I felt vulnerable and in need of affection. Although I never fully succumbed to Churchfield's lewd advances, he did force me to touch his genitals. Within days of this incident, Jo-Ann invaded the privacy of my diary, where I had recorded his inappropriate advances, and she told my father about it. He showed up at the Churchfield home with a baseball bat. The McKeesport police were called, but they did nothing consequential. The incident did seem to persuade Churchfield to keep away from me. My babysitting job was a lost cause. Later, when I was abducted, Churchfield was a prime suspect, but he passed a polygraph test while admitting his perverted advance. He was never prosecuted.

Despite that incident, I showed up at Churchfield's home weeks later, desperate once again to escape my father and Jo-Ann. At this point, Churchfield was wary. He figured that his house would be the first place the police would come looking for me. So when I arrived there, he sent me to his cousin's home. Then, when his police scanner revealed that the authorities were looking for me, he forced me to call my father.

"Will you let me come back to you and Jo-Ann?" I asked.

"Why should I," he replied, "after what you have done?"

I didn't know what to say. Fortunately, my grandpap, Jerry Kach Sr., was staying with my father and Jo-Ann at the time and persuaded them to allow me to return. My father was obviously frustrated. When I came home, the first thing he did was instruct me to call my grandmother.

"She's worried sick," he said. In typical fashion, he did not bother to ask me about my feelings or why I ran away.

As if I did not have enough to deal with, I continually guarded myself against sexual predators. Once more in late 1995, I ran away from Jo-Ann McGuire's McKeesport home. This time, no one would take me in, so I called my father and Jo-Ann. When no one answered the phone, I called Aunt Cindy, my mother's sister, to ask for help. Aunt Cindy sent her husband, Uncle Greg. He must have weighed four hundred pounds. Tattoos festooned his body from limb to limb. A long, black beard and hair completed his biker appearance.

After I entered his car, he told me that the passenger door did not open from the inside. I thought that was weird. Then, he showed me a loaded gun jammed into the waist of his pants. This terrified me. Next, he talked about his lack of sex with Aunt Cindy because she had multiple sclerosis. The conversation went downhill from there. Uncle Greg told me that he paid prostitutes for sex. He even claimed that he had paid my mom for a blowjob. Finally, he shocked me by saying that he used to masturbate while looking at a picture of me. He pulled off the road into a secluded area.

I'm going to die, I thought. All I could think to say was, "Uncle Greg, I don't feel about you that way. I think of you as a father figure."

Somehow this disarmed him.

"Oh, okay," he said and drove me the rest of the way home. Shaken from the incident, I exited the car from the driver's side, believing I had just cheated death.

When I look back at all I had to endure as a teenager, I'm reminded of the cover to my diary, where I placed a sticker that looked something like this:

"EXCUSE NOTE

Please Excuse

<u>Tanya</u>
(name)

FOREVER!
Mr. ... ...
SCHOOL PRINCIPLE"

I now understand why I related to the idea of an "EXCUSE FOREVER!"

I hated my parents' divorce, the relocation to a new school, Jo-Ann's hostility, and the way men treated me as a sex object. My spirituality remained my only hope in life. I thought my prayers had been answered in late 1995, when Thomas Hose, a security guard at my new school, appeared interested in me. Before I truly understood the trap in which I was ensnared, I found myself held captive by Hose in February 1996. Salvation and comfort were more than a decade away.

THE ABDUCTOR

Thomas John Hose was born in McKeesport, Pennsylvania, on November 11, 1957, in the same Soles Street home where he ultimately abused and held me captive for so many years. Although I didn't know this at the time we met, he did not graduate from high school. A life-long resident of McKeesport, he was nevertheless very much an outsider. Police officers were kings in his eyes because of the power they wielded. Even in McKeesport, where the city of Pittsburgh meets the fringe of Appalachia, a man lacking a high school education could not join the force. So he lied on his application to a private security company and somehow got a job as a pseudo police officer. The security company neither checked his references or educational background nor performed a drug-screening test.

He possessed no prior working experience whatsoever. Although he previously attended cosmetology school in order to meet women, he never worked in a salon. Other than dealing drugs, the security guard position was the first job he had held in his thirty-plus years of life. He was assigned to Cornell Intermediate School in 1994, one year before I began attending.

Our first encounter occurred a few weeks after I started eighth grade at Cornell. At the end of the school day, I left my math class early to retrieve a project from woodshop and prepare for the ride home on the school bus. Thomas Hose approached me and I thought I was in for trouble. Monica Krimm and other girls had already warned me that he was mean and nasty. In his midthirties, he was only about five feet eight, with a thick moustache, brown eyes, and coarse, black hair, which we guessed was dyed. Like most of the security guards at the school, he was not in the best shape.

When he stopped me that day, he asked for my hall pass. I gave it to him, and he cracked a joke. I giggled. Despite what the other girls said about him, I thought that he was nice.

Following this initial meeting, he frequently smiled and said hello when we encountered each other in the halls of Cornell. Then he began stopping me to ask how my day was going. As time went on, I noticed him walking past my classrooms, and we began talking regularly in the halls about any number of subjects. During these encounters, he demonstrated a genuine interest in me and asked many questions about my troubled home life. He was a good listener. When I talked about Jo-Ann and her tyrannical way, he was compassionate. I could tell by the questions he asked that he was aware of a lot about my life.

"How do you know so much about me?" I asked him once.

"I'm a security guard," he said. "It's my job to know everything about everyone in the school."

Still, I was flattered. The more time I spent with him, I began to feel as if my company was important to him. By contrast, I never felt important to my father, my mom, or Jo-Ann. He told me I could call him "Tom," and as we began to bond, I developed a crush on him. My feelings were driven, not by his physical appearance, but by the way he seemed to genuinely care about me.

He provided me with the attention and affection I so desperately craved.

He told me that he was also an only child and that he had "flipped out" over his father's cheating. For many years, Bud Hose arrived home from work, ate dinner, and waited for the phone to ring. The phone rang just one time, without anyone picking it up, and Bud flew out the door.

"Finally, I had enough and beat the shit out of him," he said. "After that, no more phone calls. I don't even know if the bastard is my father anyway."

"Then who is?" I asked.

"A guy named Gene, maybe. He used to visit my mom and me for the longest time. Then they got into an argument of some kind, and I never saw him again until his funeral."

That broke my heart. I wasn't the only one who had problems at home. At least I knew who my parents were. As the school year progressed, I could no longer contain my emotions. I wrote him a note telling him how I felt. When he saw me the day after I gave it to him, he wore a big smile on his face. I continued writing notes to him. He said that he was flattered and encouraged me to keep sending them.

"When will you be sending more?" he would ask. "I look forward to your letters."

In one of the notes, I wrote, "I love you." It was like writing in my diary the way I had done when I had developed crushes on other boys. Only this time, someone was actually reading my words. Someone, I thought, who cared about me.

Soon I started cutting classes so I could walk the halls of Cornell with him whenever possible. I felt comfortable sharing the details of my unhappy life in Jo-Ann McGuire's McKeesport home. This was the first time since I had moved to McKeesport that I felt as if I mattered to someone and that someone actually cared about me.

As my home life became worse, he did even more to make me feel important.

By this time, I was involved in fights with other girls at Cornell. They claimed I was talking about them behind their backs or that I was looking at their boyfriends. Although I never instigated these encounters, when pushed, I defended myself and pushed back. Tom Hose did his best to see that I avoided punishment. The same was true when he would catch me skipping school. As long as no other faculty or staff member was involved in breaking up a fight or catching me skipping class, I was able to avoid the consequences.

I realize now how obvious my crush must have been to everyone else. Rumors began to spread among faculty, staff, and students about our relationship. After only a few short months at Cornell, I followed Tom Hose everywhere throughout the school, and our interaction was caught on school video cameras and viewed by our principal, Mrs. Abrams.

She was filling in for the regular principal due to an illness and apparently did not know what to do about the security guard and the troubled teen walking the halls of Cornell past teachers and administrators daily and on multiple occasions. We continued our constant companionship and were always together at school. Other kids teased me. People said Tom Hose was a control-freak, that he was "buggy" and "a wannabe." He wore his clothes too tight, they pointed out. He reeked of cologne. They even said he flirted with students and staff members and touched women in offensive ways. I was too naïve to recognize his behavior as inappropriate, and I didn't care what others said about his appearance and personality. I knew Tom Hose cared about me, and that was more important than what people thought of him. I openly boasted to the other kids about our relationship.

I later learned that Mrs. Abrams was aware of my crush on Tom Hose because he went to her and said I was writing him love letters. She told him she would take care of it. Instead, she continued to let him remain responsible for my discipline for fighting, skipping class, or some other behavioral problem. One day, when Mrs. Abrams directed him to expel me because of some misbehavior on my part, he even lit a cigarette for me outside the building, in full view of her.

Still, the only thing that Mrs. Abrams ever said to me about him was, "Tanya, stop hanging around Mr. Hose so much."

In a feeble effort to keep us from interacting, she finally moved my study hall from a room close to where Tom Hose was centered in the building. At the time, I was glad to get away with spending time with my crush. Today, I cannot fathom how the school staff deliberately ignored what was occurring right in front of their faces.

I continued to get in trouble, and sometimes I ended up in the office of Dan Pacella, the assistant principal at Cornell. With black, stringy hair covering a shiny bald spot, he was known as "Comb-over Dan." A former basketball coach, he had no administrative certificate from the Pennsylvania Department of Education, which is required by law. Of course, I did not know that at the time. Nor did I know that Tom Hose had discussed with Pacella the rumors and love letters regarding himself and me. However, Mr. Pacella never intervened and never reported what he knew about us to his superior.

I later learned that Tom Hose read my confidential counseling records by manipulating Debbie Burnett, the guidance counselor at Cornell. She shared with him the difficulties I had experienced in my transition from Monongahela to McKeesport. Prior to my abduction, I had participated in group therapy with Ms. Burnett and others. She freely told this man—a school security guard— about my mom's mental breakdown and the abuse she subjected me to, as well as the inappropriate advances I had to fend off from Kevin Churchfield and Uncle Gregg. She talked about the feelings of despair I was experiencing, particularly under the "Rules for Living," directives that Jo-Ann had plastered on her refrigerator. No wonder I felt that Tom Hose knew me so well. He had gotten his information from the source.

Even upon enrolling in Cornell, I had serious academic problems, and Ms. Burnett knew it, just as she knew about my conflicts at home. As the school year progressed, I continued to demonstrate poor academic skills. Many of my absences during the 1995-1996 school year were unexcused. Although Ms. Burnett identified me as an at-risk student, she did not refer me to the student assistance program mandated for at-risk students by Pennsylvania law. Although she was responsible for team staffing with the school's professional personnel to monitor student progress and plan future courses of action, that did not happen in my case. I learned all of this later, and it has helped me better understand why Tom Hose was able to make me believe that no one cared about what happened to me. It was because no one did.

As the faculty and staff at Cornell doomed my education, and as Tom Hose manipulated Ms. Burnett, Mrs. Abrams, and Mr. Pacella, my behavior grew worse, and the McKeesport police ineffectively intervened. Juvenile Lieutenant E. Michael Elias, of the McKeesport police, was often called to Cornell for discipline issues involving many different students, and Tom Hose always pointed me out to him.

According to Elias, Tom Hose once told him: "That's Tanya Kach. She's got lots of problems, but she likes to come on to older men," he told Elias. "One time, she even tried to get me into trouble by saying I tried to molest her or ask her on a date."

Outside of school, I began calling Tom Hose to discuss the despair I felt about my parents' separation and just to talk. At the age of thirty-eight, he was still living with his parents, as he had almost all of his life except for the brief period while he was married. When I called, sometimes his mother, Eleanor, would answer the phone, but she would not ask too many questions. I knew that was because he dominated his parents. He had told me they were terrified of him.

If he was not there, his mother would ask who was calling so she could give him a message. I did as Tom Hose had instructed me to and replied, "Just a friend. I'll call back."

Around this time, Tom Hose actually allowed my friend Brandy Donkin and me to visit him at his Soles Street home. We went there one day after school. Our encounter with him was brief, and we chatted awhile on his front porch.

Back in school, he gave me money, candy, and cigarettes. For Christmas of 1995, he bought me a necklace. Soon after, Monica Krimm ripped it off my neck in a fight that Tom Hose had to break up. After this fight, as he escorted me, he noticed that one of my fingers was bleeding. He kissed my finger and gave me a hug. Again, I felt safe and protected, and my dependency on him grew even greater. I had no idea that my abduction was weeks away.

RUNAWAY AND THE ROAD TO RUIN

On January 2, 1996, Tom Hose discovered my secret hiding place under a stairwell in the Cornell gymnasium. Originally, I discovered it when I was cutting class, and I shared it with some of my new girlfriends at Cornell. There, we would cut class together and smoke cigarettes. On that day in January, Tom Hose found me there with another Cornell student. He immediately directed the other student to the office to be disciplined for cutting class and smoking inside the school.

We were alone together, hidden, and what happened next was like a scene from a movie. We both gazed into each other's eyes and, seemingly in slow motion, moved toward each other as I fell into his arms, and he kissed and caressed me passionately. Time stopped for a moment. Suddenly, a school bell rang, and he had to resume his duties. In the time that followed, before I began my captivity with him in February 1996, we would meet in that secret stairwell several more times. For me, these make-out sessions made me feel as if I were the most important person in the world. My home life continued in turmoil, and I was constantly running away. But with Tom Hose, I felt a refuge from the turmoil.

As I shared with him my experiences of trying to escape my father and Jo-Ann, he encouraged me to run away and helped me with specific instructions on the two bus routes I would have to travel to arrive in Charleroi if my aunt Susie was not able to give me a ride. He also gave me money for the bus to get there.

On the particular occasion when he directed and funded my runaway to my maternal grandmother, my mom was summoned and arrived to take me to meet her new boyfriend, Craig Koehnke, who ultimately became her second husband. Craig, a successful contractor, had no polish at all and was what the kids at school would call a douche bag. An unattractive bald man, he yammered on and dominated a conversation with ignorant opinions and bewildering comments about odd and unusual subjects, such as a woman he once knew who was sexually abused. He was also very controlling of my mom. On top of my discontent with Jo-Ann, I felt great pain realizing that my mom was dating someone else, especially an idiot like Craig.

Later, I was less harsh with my assessment of him. All the same, upon meeting Craig and arriving at his home, I called Tom Hose that same day to let him know that I had made it to my mom according to plan. But there was no way that Craig was going to let my mom and me stay with him. Given her cramped living arrangements with my grandmother and Aunt Susie, Mom had no choice but to reject my request to live with her. She returned me to my father and Jo-Ann in McKeesport.

Though this was just another time she had rejected my requests to live with her, it also served as a precursor to my prolonged captivity. Because Tom Hose had become so involved with my running away, he came to see how futile it was for me to try. He said he had a better way to save me from Jo-Ann.

Meanwhile, time and time again, I tried to escape to my grandmother's Charleroi home. Always, I would call my mom to pick me up there, and always, I would be returned to McKeesport. Every time I ran away, my father called the police. Even if my mom had not been one of three people sharing a one-bedroom apartment or living out of her car, she was obligated by court order to return me to my father. Sometimes, she would not even take me as far as Jo-Ann's house. Rather, in the dark of night, I would be set out on a street corner convenient to wherever it was that she was headed.

The second-to-last time I ran away was Super Bowl Sunday, January 28, 1996. I was gone for ten days and stayed for the first time with Tom Hose. In addition to his parents, Bud and Eleanor, he also lived with Justin, his son from his failed marriage. His parents were away that Super Bowl Sunday, and he had agreed to allow me to hide out there. "Keep your mouth shut about her," he told Justin, his son, and Justin nodded in silent agreement.

"He never disobeys his father," Tom Hose said.

The inside of his house was not what I had expected. I thought that it would be warm and cozy. Instead, it was outdated and uninviting. The telephone was rotary. The furniture was covered with sheets. Later that day, for the first time, he took me to the bedroom that would become my cage for years to come.

It was a wood-paneled space, about the size of three prison cells. As we entered the only door into the room, I saw a full-sized bed pressed against the opposite end between two narrow windows. On the right side of the bed, a box sat under the window between the bed and a dresser on the far right wall. The box was there to hold my meager belongings, and the dresser contained Justin's things. Justin slept on the floor in a body-sized space next to what became my side of the bed.

Sitting on the bed and looking across on the opposite wall between the doorway and a closet door, I saw a television and stereo. The walls were adorned mostly with sports memorabilia, such as a pen-and-ink drawing of Roberto Clemente, the Pittsburgh Pirates baseball player whose untimely death Tom Hose had always been obsessed with. Posters depicting various hockey players who played for the Pittsburgh Penguins were taped up all over the place. A large poster of John Lennon, another of his obsessions, hung on the wall.

That Super Bowl Sunday was the first night I spent there. Soon, we were making out, and he was telling me how good it was that I was with him and how wonderful it felt to hold and fondle me.

"I don't want to let you go," he said. "Why don't you just spend the night?"

And I did. *Why not?* I thought. I had a history of running away, and he was right when he said, "They don't care anyway."

That night, I felt wanted and loved so much more so than I did in Jo-Ann's home.

The next day, when he went to work, he left me behind in his bedroom by myself. I already knew the rules for staying with him, and I followed them. I remained in the bedroom with the door locked from the inside, so that when his parents returned, they could not enter. For obvious reasons, he did not want them to find out that he, at age thirty-eight, was harboring a fourteen-year-old girl in his bedroom. I could not even leave to use the bathroom and was ultimately provided with a bucket for a chamber pot the next day. The evening following the Super Bowl and the day that followed, I went twenty hours without relief. To this day, I have flashbacks when I see a bucket. Over the years, there were three of them: beige, blue, and red.

When I heard his parents come upstairs, I secreted myself even farther, into the bedroom closet. That first day, after he left for work, I locked myself into that bedroom and thought of the way that Jo-Ann had taken the door off of my room. At last, I had privacy, and I felt safe.

Because I could not make any noise that might alert his parents that I was there, I memorized the floor boards that creaked and avoided them with my life. A square-foot area by the corner of Justin's dresser by the closet squeaked the most. Also, the furnace vent on the floor, near where Tom Hose kept the makeshift toilet bucket was way too noisy if I stepped on it. On my side of the bed, the middle of the floor made a small creaking noise if I stepped on it a certain way. The bed itself made terrible noise if I did not sit down on it gently.

Tuesday or Wednesday after the Super Bowl, Tom Hose introduced me to his friend Judy Sokol. She was separated and living with her two adult children, Brandon and Season, while in the midst of a divorce from her husband, Bob, a former McKeesport police officer.

Bob's friendship with Tom Hose grew in intensity as Bob Sokol battled child rape charges, and Tom Hose provided emotional support through Bob's criminal trial for the charges. Following a mistrial, Bob had pled "no contest" to indecent assault on a minor and was sentenced to probation in a saga that spread from the late 1980s through the early 1990s. During this period, he had run for mayor of McKeesport but, not surprisingly, lost and was then thrown out as police chief by his rival for violating a law that prohibited a police officer from running for elected office.

Despite the Sokols' divorce, Tom Hose had managed to remain friends with both Bob and Judy. She lived about four blocks away and worked as a hair stylist. A heavy-set woman, Judy wore lots of makeup and bright lip gloss. She had big red hair teased out wildly and held with cans of hair spray.

"This is Tanya," Tom Hose said.

"Wonderful to meet you," she replied and gave me a big hug.

That kind gesture warmed my heart. My parents never hugged me, and Jo-Ann saw me as a thing that neither deserved nor needed affection. Meeting Judy was a happy moment in my unsettled life.

After Tom Hose introduced us, he and Judy went to an upstairs bedroom in Judy's house for about half an hour while I remained in the living room watching television. When they returned, he told me, "Judy's going to help you escape the situation at Jo-Ann's. You can stay here with her while I'm at work."

"Thank you," I said, uncertain about how long this situation would work.

"Now, that's settled," Judy said. "Let's order a pizza."

During those first days that I spent time with Judy, I told her all about my situation. Judy was compassionate in her response to the way I described the abuse I suffered at the hands of Jo-Ann and my father, as well as my mom's mental illness. Even so, after ten days, Judy seemingly realized that what was going on with Tom Hose was not appropriate behavior.

"Go to your mom again," she said.

"But she doesn't have room for me."

"She'll make the room once you tell her what's happening," Judy told me. "Honey, it's not right to live the way you are."

"Okay," I said to myself as well as to her. "I'll try."

Unable to reach Aunt Susie for a ride, I called my mother's sister, Aunt Cindy. Her husband, Greg, picked me up from a convenience store near Judy's house.

This was the time when my uncle Greg tried to rape me. Once I contacted my mom, she sent me back to my father and Jo-Ann's home. Close to tears, I told them about the attempted rape by Uncle Greg.

Jo-Ann sighed. "You're lying."

"I'm not lying." I turned to my father. "It really happened. I was scared to death."

He shook his head. "You need to stop making up stories for attention, Tanya," he said.

This time, I stayed with my father for just four days. I would not see him again for more than a decade.

I was not as much running away from my father as much as I was Jo-Ann. By most measures, the relationship between my father and me was not hostile, just distant because he worked so much and did not have any interest in parenting. I resented Jo-Ann and felt like an outsider in her home. Jo-Ann was hot-headed and did not exhibit any tolerance for the difficulties I was experiencing. And often, when I ran away, my father handled the situation poorly. My adjustment problems continued to propel me toward my mom. I couldn't help trying to run back to her.

> Dear Mommy, Hello how are you. I'm fine I guess. I haven't seen you in a while. You made no effort to see me, did you? You have to understand, you and daddy are divorced for good. I don't like it either. You gotta talk to daddy about visitation. But I know I'll definitely see you on my birthday because it's on a Saturday. Did you get me anything? Well tell Grandma and Grampe & Susie & Cindy I said Hi and love them, c-ya.
>
> Love Always,
> Your daughter
> Tanya 4-ever and always. No one
> Will ever take your place.

That February of 1996, when my mom rejected me in response to Judy Sokol's suggestion that I turn to her one last time, the die was cast. Tom Hose talked Judy into taking me back, and I ran away to her home on February 10, 1996.

The night before, I packed my belongings in a book bag and hid it behind the furnace in the basement of Jo-Ann's home. Then I set my alarm to wake me early the next morning. When I woke up, I discovered that Jo-Ann was already awake. Although this upset me, I decided to go while Jo-Ann was in the shower. After dressing, I went down to the basement to get my book bag. While I was there, I dropped my pajamas at the bottom of the basement stairs. As I packed my book-bag, I caught a glimpse of Jo-Ann watching; she must have known that I was leaving. Surely she would tell my father as much. Then I climbed the stairs and walked out the back door of Jo-Ann's house into an unimaginable ordeal.

FIRST PERIOD OF CAPTIVITY

Looking back, I can see that my captivity and abuse break down into four distinct periods. First, from February 10, 1996, during approximately the first month I entered into this ordeal, I was staying comfortably at the home of Judy Sokol, ferrying back and forth between there and the Hose residence when circumstances permitted. From March 1996 through about June of 2000, I was in total seclusion at the Hose residence, during which time I did not leave the house. Next, and after I turned eighteen, from June 2000 until approximately June 2005, I experienced a quasi-seclusion. I was allowed out of the Soles Street residence on orchestrated, cloaked, and rare occasions to shop for clothing or for other reasons that would seem mundane to most people. Finally, for approximately the last ten months of my time there, I assumed an alias and was on my way to escaping.

During my first stage of captivity, I was convinced that Tom Hose was in love with me. His nickname for me was "TC," which stood for "Totally Cute." His affection for and connection to me was so well known that Monica Krimm later said, "We all knew he was doing her."

Of course, Monica was wrong. It was only after I ran away for the last time, in February 1996, that I, at the age of fourteen, lost my virginity to Tom Hose on a futon in Judy's bedroom. Prior to that time, we engaged in frequent make-out sessions at Cornell under the gymnasium stairwell, and he had groped me in almost every conceivable way. Still, up to that point, I remained a virgin, although he did not believe me when I told him so.

That night on Judy's futon, he was drunk and demanding, and I could no longer deny him. Finally, I surrendered. I was absolutely frightened by the experience, terrified that I was breaking my promise to God, and I was in physical pain. The fear must have been evident on my face, because tears welled up in Tom Hose's eyes, but he held them back and did not actually cry. Then he passed out so quickly that he slept through the night without even removing the condom he was wearing.

When he woke the next morning, he noticed blood on the condom and told me, "Wow, you were a virgin after all."

"That's what I've been trying to make you understand," I replied through trembling lips.

I felt remorse for having broken the contract I made at Bible camp. I felt that I had betrayed God and feared that I would be condemned to hell. These are the only thoughts I remember during that first sexual encounter and afterward.

Planning to keep me for good, Tom Hose had Judy alter my appearance twice. First, she dyed my hair red. I'm convinced she did this knowing that he would be annoyed, because his ex-wife had red hair. As expected, he hated the color after Judy's first make over and had her add blond highlights.

We spent lots of time together at Judy's house during the next month. He also called her to send me down to his house when his parents were out so that I could spend the night there with him. They lived within walking distance from each other and, incredibly, right near a church parking lot where McKeesport police were known to caucus before, during, and after shift changes.

But in March of 1996, my arrangement with Tom Hose and Judy Sokol changed. A state agency, then known as Children and Youth Services (CYS), was charged with investigating a Dependency Petition that my father had filed after my last disappearance in February 1996. He truly believed that my mom knew where I was and was hiding me. He even believed that CYS would take me from my mom and return me to him. I know now that many of my father's actions in the wake of my final assent into captivity were motivated by his hatred for my mom. He even had the police search the home of her then-boyfriend, now-husband, Craig Koehnke, to no avail.

This state agency was duty bound in the wake of my father's petition to make sure that, if I was ever found, I would be deemed a dependent of the state. I would not be returned immediately to the environment from which I had fled and been abducted. As part of its investigation, and based on information provided to them by my family, CYS contacted Judy about my whereabouts and whether she had any knowledge or involvement in the disappearance.

Judy freaked out. She called Tom Hose and told him that I was not welcome in her home anymore. All of this time, I was spending many nights and days in the Hose residence and following the rigid regimen necessary to avoid being detected by his parents. I looked forward to the times that I was able to get away to Judy's house. When I slept over at her place, it was easy for me to overlook her obnoxious snoring, for we shared girl talk—the kind of clothes she liked, how long it took to do her hair and make-up. I even trusted Judy enough to tell her about the intimate details of my relationship with Tom Hose. Almost incredibly, at some point prior to the involvement of CYS, Judy actually seemed happy for me. Until she could no longer overlook the blatantly illegal way in which I was being abused, she was an excellent listener, and she was kind to me. I really liked her, and I was upset to learn that I could not return to her home. Thus, my total sequestration began.

For the more than four years that followed, I never appeared outside of the Hose residence on Soles Street. During the long days, while Tom Hose and his son, Justin, were away at school, I would position myself in a slant of sunlight that traveled through the windows in the bedroom and across the bed and floor. I passed countless hours alone in that bedroom. Tom Hose's parents were oblivious to my presence there—or pretended to be. I prayed to God for guidance all the while. Otherwise, I watched television, listening to it through earphones, and read *Cat Fancy* magazine, as well as *Goosebumps* and other books. I found a spot where I could quietly exercise by doing stomach crunches.

Most of the time, I ate peanut butter and jelly sandwiches, along with a banana and a can of Faygo soda pop. Sometimes, Tom Hose smuggled me leftovers from his dinner. About twice a week, in the dead of night and after his parents were long asleep, he led me down into a cellar with cold, concrete floors to take a shower. I was fine with it at first. I thought I was in love and felt my sacrifices were a labor of my love for Tom Hose. Soon, however, the ordeal began to take its toll.

In the months that followed, I became anorexic. I lost thirty pounds, and at one point, weighed only ninety-three pounds. It took me nearly a year to overcome this affliction by forcing myself to eat when I did not possess any hunger. In addition, I began to suffer from psoriasis, which went untreated because I did not receive any medical treatment at all during my captivity.

The psoriasis was so bad that I have permanent scars from it. I suffered constant headaches, chest pains, and toothaches. Dental fillings fell out.

"Deal with it," Tom Hose told me.

When I contracted lice in late 1996, he informed me, in a matter-of-fact way, that he was thinking of killing me and dumping my body in the river.

"If Justin or I get lice, you're as good as dead," he said. In reality, either he or Justin must have already had lice without knowing it and gave it to me as I had no contact with anyone other than them in months.

I was so petrified that I decided to write a last will and testament of sorts.

One afternoon, while father and son were away at Cornell and after this threat to my life, I wrote my simple will. I wanted to make sure that if Tom Hose killed me, there was a chance that people might know who I was. So I wrote down where I was from and identified my mother and father by name, as well as my own name. I wanted to make sure that, if my body was found, I would not be cremated. For reasons even I don't fully understand, this was very important to me. I then folded the paper really small and stashed it under the carpet in Tom Hose's bedroom closet. It would stay there for years.

Not surprisingly, toward the end of my first several months in captivity, I wanted out. As my birthday and the Thanksgiving and Christmas holidays approached, I lost my appetite and became anorexic, and in early October 1996, as I was feeling sick, I decided to leave. I gathered my belongings, mustered the courage to confront Hose when he came home from work, and told him of my decision. Although I did not know where I would go, and I feared being homeless, I was finding fewer and fewer ways to keep myself from going crazy in such isolation.

He reacted by pointing in my face and saying, "If you ever try to leave me, I will kill you."

Later, he brought up the murders of two local girls that made me even more fearful. Had he murdered them? Would he do the same to me?

In any event, this particular threat against my life was not as casual as the threats he'd made when I had lice or when he spoke of killing himself, his ex-wife, and her boyfriend. Now, he was angry, truly angry, and I was terrified. Furthermore, I knew that this wasn't the first time he had effectively threatened someone's life. He had told me that, when he split from his ex-wife, he maintained custody of Justin by warning her that he would have her killed if she ever fought him over custody. I knew that he planned to murder both her and her boyfriend someday, so I stayed put. My family did not care about me. They weren't even looking for me. I could not bear the thought of being on the streets with Tom Hose tracking me down.

Later in my ordeal, he developed pink eye, and soon thereafter, I had it too, but the only remedy he gave me was Visine eye drops. The condition became so bad that I could not open my eyes. I suffered this way for more than two weeks before nature took its course and cleared up my condition. This is believed to have damaged my vision. Even when he would infect me with the flu, I would suffer without treatment and was relegated to a bucket, vomiting repeatedly for hours on end. During my worse ailments, Tom Hose banished me to the closet. I was sick and frightened that my heaving and coughing would reveal me to his parents.

Summer in that bedroom was unbearable. All we had to cool ourselves down was a box fan. Still, the temperature in that room would rise over 100 degrees. I knew this because Hose's son, Justin, was really interested in weather. He had a clock radio that also gauged humidity, barometric pressure, and temperature. Though Tom Hose could come home from work on a hot summer day and take a cool shower, I was denied such relief. Those first few years, every summer, he would make false promises to me that I could go out late at night onto the glider on the back porch and cool off. Summer after summer, he broke these promises, and I suffered in roasting heat. Then I would cry, and he would yell at me to stop. Nothing was anything close to the way I wanted it to be.

Despite how life with him was destroying me physically and mentally, I was continually torn by my plight in conflicting ways. After all, I was the center of attention for the first time in my life. Tom Hose adored me in these early years. My misguided love for him only grew as did my belief that, without him, I would be out on the street, homeless, or dead. In addition, I was not without the companionship of someone close to my age and interests. That someone was Justin Hose.

JUSTIN

Because Tom Hose introduced his son to me from the outset, and because Justin maintained his father's secret unfailingly, we eventually became friends. Justin hated me at first, but he warmed up over time. We discovered that we had been students at Cornell at the same time. Justin was in sixth grade there when I transferred to Cornell to begin eighth grade. Back then, he was a fat, shy kid, a loner with no friends at all until later in life, when he started dating women. He once weighed 240 pounds but later dropped down to 180. Although he was a good student, Justin was not involved in any extracurricular activities at school. Still, while captive in the Hose household, I spent my days alone while Justin and Tom Hose were in school (and later when Justin graduated from school and had a job), but when Justin came home, he and I would play all sorts of video games together, mostly sports games on his PlayStation 1. When he was there, I no longer had to use headphones, but I still had to keep my voice down.

We shared many long, quiet conversations. Sometimes we would just bounce a ball back and forth from spots across the bedroom where we sat on the floor. I also paid attention to Justin's interest in meteorology and watched the weather radar with him on television. We played checkers and Monopoly, watched all sorts of television programs together, and generally passed the time. Over the years, I would make cards for Justin on his birthday. Later on, during the third period of my captivity, when I was allowed out on clandestine and rare occasions, I bought him junk food and candy. Tom Hose described my relationship with his son as, "Like brother and sister," in a deposition he gave in connection with legal proceedings that followed my escape from him. In all honesty, for quite some time, Justin was good company for me, but he always had his baggage.

For starters, he was emotionless. He rarely shared his feelings and did not like to talk about anything of substance. He hated his mother, and I remember him mentioning her only once. That day he came home and told his father that he had run into her.

"That slut came up to talk to me, and I said, 'Fuck you, bitch,' and walked away."

His father laughed and said, "That's my boy."

I was taken aback by his comments. Justin was completely brainwashed against his mother by his father, who would constantly tell him that his mother was a slut and a whore who left them for another man. Likewise, Justin was brainwashed against Bud Hose, his grandfather, but he got along fine with his grandmother, Eleanor. Again because his father made it so.

Justin could be so cold and distant that, even when I told him that his father threatened my life, he was silent. And I did tell him everything, from the way his father and I hooked up to what had been going on in Jo-Ann's McKeesport home. Justin just shrugged. On a couple of occasions, he even witnessed me packing my belongings when I considered leaving, but again, he had no response at all.

When he was questioned by the police in 2006 after my rescue, he stated that he did not want to be involved but confirmed that I had been living in the Soles Street home with him, his grandparents, and his father since I was fourteen. He also confirmed that his grandparents were unaware of this fact because he was a private individual and was told not to say anything. He commented that no one really understood the situation and that it was better for me to live with them than with Jo-Ann. He stated that we would often talk about my home life, which was terrible. My father and Jo-Ann did not care about me, he said, and I was better off living with his father. Despite some grains of truth in all of this, obviously, Justin was as delusional as Tom Hose.

Despite his comments to the police, during the later phase of my total sequestration in that Soles Street bedroom, and as I began to mature into a young woman, Justin showed how his father's traits appeared in him as a case of the acorn falling close to the tree. Sometime in 1999, he began to walk in on me when I was changing my clothes. Eventually, he propositioned me for sex. Sometimes before that, he and I would wrestle around, but that stopped when Justin tried to cop a feel of my breasts. He even offered me bribes. "Show me your tits," he would beg.

Once, when Bud and Eleanor were away, and Justin and I were cleaning up together in the basement, I became frightened by a spider. Justin came up behind me and grabbed my breasts, proclaiming, "We have to protect these."

I was able to resist him by letting him know that I would tell his father if he tried anything. Justin never got what he really wanted, though he never ceased propositioning me until later on, when he had a girlfriend. Then, just like his father, Justin was pursuing women where he worked. So, my circumstances were so bizarre that I had to guard my honor for a man I thought I loved against the advances of that man's son. Even though I found Justin's advances repugnant, he had been the only human being with whom I could interact, other than his father, for those first four years. I felt conflicted and confused about him. My troubled mind began to suffer greatly as I faced complete subjugation in increasingly abnormal ways.

Not only did I feel powerless against my insistence that every item in Tom Hose's bedroom be relegated to a place, but I also became fixated on numbers. Inexplicably, I was enslaved into fearing the numbers three, six, eight, nine, and thirteen. Any time I did anything any one of these numbers of noises caused me to repeat myself so that I experienced a safe number of noises. Opening and closing a drawer, for example, was such a ritual for me. Much as was the case with my anorexia, I had to will myself not to engage in countless counting, but it took years for me to master my own mental faculties in this regard.

My obsessive-compulsive disorder and my anorexia, as well as my devolving state of mental health, served to preclude me from rational thinking. In the absence of anyone or anything else to guide me in this situation, it was the only life I came to know. And what I knew of this life, I made the most of. Almost every day in that room, for nine of the ten years I spent there, was identical. I woke each morning at the same time as Tom Hose and Justin as they readied themselves and left for the day. I locked the bedroom door behind them after they left and then said my prayers. After that, I watched morning television programs—*Good Morning America*, followed by *Live With Regis and Kelly*. In the afternoon, I listened to the radio and read magazines as I waited for Justin and his father to return. As I waited, I listened for the sounds of people walking up the stairs outside the bedroom and then peered under the door to recognize the shoes as Justin's or his father's. When I was certain it was one of them, I would unlock the door.

For the entire time of my captivity, I never dared to watch television or listen to the radio without earphones unless Justin or his father was in the room, as I never abandoned my fear that

Eleanor and Bud would discover me in their son's room. And so it was that I was mute in my interaction with the world. While interacting with the world on television or radio, I was deaf to that going on around me. Only when I ventured to take the headphones off to read or when I was otherwise listening to conversations through ventilation ducts or interacting in whispers with Tom Hose or Justin did I experience a half-stilted existence. Otherwise, I was in a sort of sound chamber. When not, I was nowhere anyone would really recognize. The days passed in surreal similarity as I waited for my situation to somehow change, day after day after day.

In addition, there were sex rituals and other means by which Tom Hose had me answer to his every whim. I learned to cherish certain other moments.

For instance, every third Thursday of the month during most of my ordeal, Tom Hose's parents went to senior meetings. These were social gatherings sponsored by the Catholic Church from 6:15 until about 8:30 in the evenings. On those nights, I could roam the Hose residence at will. This became bath night, the one time when I was not hurried down into the basement for a shower in the middle of the night. For most of my ordeal, and for more than nine years, this was the only night I could enjoy the luxury of a warm bath. For my sixteenth birthday, all I desired was a warm bath, but it was not a Thursday. Except for the chocolate éclair that Tom Hose gave me for my birthday that year, it was a sad day for me. Still, I loved Thursday nights.

"YOU ARE MY PROPERTY."

Regardless of the behavior I developed to deal with my captivity, I found my judgment constantly challenged. This was made more difficult by the fact that I came from such a dysfunctional family. I had never been too certain what "normal" was, but I was now trying desperately to hang onto what I thought I knew of it. Although I understood my circumstances were bizarre at the very least—and although I was afraid of Tom Hose—I was well aware that my survival depended on adapting. Adapt I did. I spent my first four Christmas holidays in Tom Hose's bedroom closet.

With the exception of one year when Bob Sokol visited on Christmas Eve, all I knew of the Hose Christmas holiday celebration was limited to Tom Hose, Justin, Bud, and Eleanor. No one else ever shared the holiday with the family during the decade I was there. Every year, they kept their gifts for each other wrapped up in their bedrooms. When Christmas Eve arrived, they had a special dinner and then shuffled up and down the stairs to bring down and exchange presents with each other one at a time.

Hiding me in his bedroom closet allowed Tom Hose to open his usually locked bedroom door. He could come in and out as he gathered his gifts. He could catch a smoke after the meal. Through the ventilations ducts, his family's conversations floated up to me. I heard them praise one another for their generosity. I listened to them speak of gratitude and joy. At these moments, which were some of my worst—when I should have been praising God and celebrating the birth of Jesus Christ—I prayed for salvation and for love.

Despite my belief that no one cared about me, my mom called the Hose residence after I had been gone a couple of months. She was upset that I had placed a toll call to Tom Hose from Craig Koehnke's house the time Tom Hose gave me bus route directions and money to run away to Charleroi. His telephone number appeared on Craig's telephone bill, so my mom contacted Tom Hose to see if he knew anything about the call and about my disappearance.

"I don't even know your daughter," he told her.

To me, he said, "The only reason she called is because she's upset about the cost of the phone call. She doesn't give a damn about what happened to you."

I had heard only one side of the conversation and believed him. *After all*, I told myself, *if my family was really interested in finding me, my mom would have done more than merely call there one time and only to ask about a phone bill.*

I had no way of knowing that my mom had reported this charge on Craig's phone bill to the McKeesport police or that the police had done nothing. Tom Hose insisted that if anyone was really looking for me, his phone number on that bill would have directed them right to me. Given the paranoia that swelled

in me during those first several months of isolation, Tom Hose was readily able to use any information about my family as poison in my mind. When no one came looking for me after my mom called him, I believed what he said—except for him, I was truly alone in the world.

Sometime in 1996, I recall a woman calling the Hose residence, claiming to his mother that I was there. The woman said that she was calling the police. Either that night or the next, at least one junior juvenile lieutenant from the McKeesport Police arrived at the Hose residence. Fortunately for Tom Hose, his parents had already gone upstairs to sleep. As he observed the police officers arrive on his porch, his immediate thoughts turned to me.

They knocked on the door. He hurriedly led me down to the basement.

"If they come in the house, you hide in there." He gestured to a large cardboard box.

I was numb, afraid to scream but thinking also that maybe my family really did care. Maybe, finally, someone would come and take me home.

In the basement, through the floorboards, I could hear the conversation between Tom Hose and the officers. At the front door, the officers asked if he knew anything about me.

"Nothing," he told them.

Well, would he permit a search of the property to prove that he was not harboring me?

He pled with the officer to spare waking his elderly parents by such an intrusion. He later told me that he invited the officer to search the entire property but that he declined to do so out of respect for his parents.

After this anonymous phone call warning Hose's parents that I was there, I allowed myself to feel hope. My faith had taught me to believe in miracles, and maybe that's what was happening.

"The police wouldn't just come here on their own," I told Tom Hose. "Maybe my family really is looking for me."

"No," he said. "That's just some old bitty in the neighborhood being a neb shit. You know your parents don't care about you."

My heart sank right along with my hopes.

At every opportunity, he degraded my family and their lack of concern for me. He constantly called me stupid. "You're just a pretty face," he would tell me. "You'll never make it on your own. You were put on this earth to take care of me, and me to take care of you."

He was fond of pointing out that, "I trained you my way." He meant sex, of course. He also meant my behavior. He had trained me not to talk back, and I never did. I also did whatever he wanted me to in bed. The message I heard day and night was, "I trained you, and you are my property."

I believed him. In my deep isolation, Tom Hose created a false reality that I quickly came to accept.

When my father and Jo-Ann bought a home in Elizabeth, Pennsylvania, he showed me the newspaper that published the public record of the deed recorded in the name of Jerry Kach and Jo-Ann McGuire.

"See," he said. "They've moved on. It's as if you never mattered to them."

He was both wrong and right, but it would take many more years for me to figure that out.

Over the next two years, however, I was unable to hide my desire to leave. When I expressed my feelings, his focus changed from threats back to his original theme that no one cared.

In 1997, he showed me the newspaper clipping that announced the marriage of Sherri and Craig Koehnke. I was devastated. My mom was remarried. She'd had a wedding, and now she had a new husband.

"She's moved on," Tom Hose said, as he had about my father. "She doesn't care about you."

Just before my sixteenth birthday, I felt as if I could not continue, regardless of the price. I knew he would probably threaten to kill me again, but even that would not stop me. I had to make him listen.

It was dark outside, and we were lying in bed. Justin was out with friends, and I knew I'd better take advantage of the opportunity to speak honestly. I looked over at him, this man I had once trusted more than anyone.

"Tom," I said, bracing myself for the threat that was sure to follow, "I need to talk to you about something. About leaving here, I mean."

He didn't hit me. Didn't threaten. Instead, he looked at me with great sadness.

"Who saved your life?"

"You," I replied, "but..."

"Who takes care of you?"

"I know that," I told him. "I just can't live like this."

"*You* can't live? What about me? You would destroy my life if you left. I am the only person to ever show you love, and you would leave me? Don't be stupid."

"Please listen to me," I said in a soft voice, so he wouldn't think I was trying to talk back.

"I've heard all I need to." His gaze bore into me, and I couldn't decipher the emotion in his eyes. "If you leave me, Tanya, I'll kill myself. I can't live without you."

Even though he had terrified me, he'd taken care of me, which was more than my parents had done. I felt both gratitude and fear, and the thought of his contemplating suicide confused me even more. How could I leave him? How could I stay?

NO ONE FINDS A MILK-CARTON KID

He didn't kill himself, and I didn't leave. Still, I kept that hope of doing so alive, and I prayed that, with God's help, I would one day walk out of this place.

Meanwhile, I was learning more and more disturbing things about the connection between Tom Hose and other former Cornell students. First, I discovered that another student at Cornell had been found dead on the banks of the Monongahela River back in 1995, when I first started attending school in McKeesport. When she was found dead, Anna Marie Callahan had been the same age as I was when Tom Hose abducted me, she resembled my appearance, and she had been subject to the authority of Tom Hose because he worked at Cornell. Anna Marie Callahan had been strangled to death. No one was ever charged with her murder. Coincidentally, just a few months after Callahan was killed, Thomas Hose, then thirty-eight years old, was kissing me under the school gymnasium stairs, in January 1996, when I was barely fourteen years old.

Then, more than two years after my captivity began with Tom Hose, in June 1998, another young girl who attended Cornell, Kimberlie Krimm, went missing. Just as with Anna Marie Callahan, Kimberlie Krimm and I were somewhat similar in appearance. Likewise, we were both the same age when we disappeared and were both subject to Tom Hose's authority as a security guard at Cornell. The badly decomposed body of Kimberlie Krimm was found in a cemetery visible from Tom Hose's Soles Street home.

At first, I learned of Kimberlie Krimm's murder from Justin, who came home one day to report it. Chills shot through me. Kimberlie Krimm was the younger sister of Monica Krimm, my first friend at Cornell, the girl who later yanked the necklace Tom Hose had given me off my neck. Now Monica's sister was dead. How could that be?

When Tom Hose was informed that Krimm had been found dead, he did not seem surprised and said, "You knew that was coming." This stuck me as an unusually strange and cold reaction to learning about a death. Tom Hose hated Kimberlie Krimm because of all of her problems at Cornell and because of my troublesome interactions with her sister. One evening, after he had been drinking, Tom Hose even described to me the configuration of Krimm's dead body as it was discovered in the cemetery. These details were especially disturbing, because no details had been reported at the time. He claimed that Krimm's lifeless body was found propped up on a hillside amidst overgrown grass and shrubbery. He further claimed that Krimm was slouched over her knees, which were bent inward and up against her chest. He went on to describe Krimm's panties being drawn down to her ankles. According to official reports, the manner and time of

Krimm's death were undetermined because her body was so badly decomposed when she was discovered by authorities.

After my rescue, while Tom Hose was in jail awaiting his trial, a jailhouse snitch claimed that Tom Hose confessed to the murder of Kimberlie Krimm. Detectives sat down with me to ask me about this. When asked, I could not recall any time when Tom Hose came home as if he had killed someone, such as with blood on his clothes. He could have showered and cleaned up without me knowing, however, because of my imprisonment in the bedroom. To this day, it haunts me to remember the way Tom Hose described Krimm's body. He claimed he knew this because the police told him. No cop has ever admitted that. Many speculate that Kimberlie Krimm was killed by Hose because she knew he was keeping me in his bedroom. No one has ever been charged with Kimberlie's murder.

Krimm's murder also served as another indication that my disappearance was receiving attention. By chance, I read a newspaper article about her death. As I read on, I was shocked to see my own name. The article went on to say that I was registered with a national database for missing children.

When Tom Hose returned from work that day, I showed the article to him and pointed at my name.

"Did you know about this?" I asked.

"No, and neither does anyone else," he replied. "All it means is that you're just another number in some data base. After all, no one ever finds a milk-carton kid."

For once, I didn't accept his explanation. Although I was conflicted between gratitude and the need for a real life, I knew the *real life* I wanted would never happen as long as we lived as we had been.

At first, he had promised me that we would move out of his parents' house and into an apartment. To prove his point, he often read the classifieds section of the *McKeesport Daily News*, telling me he was trying to find a place for us. All the same, for one reason or another, he gave me all kinds of excuses about what the apartments listed for rent lacked. They were too small, he would tell me, too large, too expensive, too cheap. On the poor side of town, in the rich part of town, too far away from his job. And always, always, too dangerous. Someone might see me there; someone could trace him. At the time, I could not understand why he never followed through on his promises about creating a life for me outside of the bedroom in his parents' house. All I knew was that I was feeling more and more drained.

In October 1998, Judy Sokol called. I had liked Judy from the moment I met her and hoped that her showing up in our lives was a good thing.

"Can I see her?" I asked him.

"She wants to talk to me alone," he said, and I could tell he was concerned. "Outside. You stay put, okay?"

I didn't talk back. Judy drove up and stopped in the alley. Tom Hose got inside her car, and they drove away. When he returned later that night, I asked him what had happened.

"She just wanted to know if you were still with me." He grinned in the dark. "I said you were long gone. Said I didn't have a clue where you are."

I quit smoking cigarettes on August 23, 1996, and managed to remain tobacco-free for the next seven years. Although Tom Hose exposed me to marijuana and alcohol almost immediately from the time I first stayed in his house, this too had an unexpectedly chance benefit. Although I had tried marijuana when Kevin Churchfield offered it to me back in 1995, I didn't like the way it made me feel. When I tried it again with Tom Hose, I was turned off for good. I don't know how it affects other people, but for me, that fragrant smoke only sank me deeper into despair.

I didn't like alcohol either, for many of the same reasons, but most of all because it enhanced my feelings of sadness and isolation. Tom Hose kept a full bottle of Jack Daniels in his bedroom at all times, but I never touched it. My alcohol limit is one drink, two at the most.

Although I rolled twenty marijuana cigarettes for him every Friday night for more than a decade, I was never once tempted to take any for myself. By contrast to his generally dark demeanor, Tom Hose was a happy drunk. Indeed, when he drank, no one could shut him up. Yet I was turned off by drugs and alcohol during my captivity. I didn't need to look to them for comfort. I had my belief in God.

My life was slow. It was depressing. For the first four years, Tom Hose did not even allow me to breathe fresh air or enjoy the light of day from anywhere except behind a window. Finally, I turned eighteen. I also entered the third phase of my captivity. It was sometime around March 2000, the beginning of a new kind of confinement for me, one where I remained secluded in the Hose residence under rigid limitations to avoid detection by and Bud and Eleanor, but also one where I finally enjoyed some sparse, secret, and ultimately welcomed exposure to the world.

It was a weekend, and Tom Hose's parents were away in Atlantic City, New Jersey. After more than four years wearing hand-me-down clothing from Tom and Justin Hose, I said that I really needed some clothes that fit.

"Okay," Tom Hose said. "We can make it work." And with that permission from my captor, I soon ventured into the outside world by myself.

and how he had "… so much power over women." My mind set was one of confusion rather than escape.

Most confusing was my need to interact with people during this shopping excursion—people on the bus, people in the department store, people in general. It was simply odd being around anyone other than Tom Hose and Justin.

On the bus, a lady must have noticed my dazed expression.

"Honey, are you on the right bus?" she asked.

I nodded yes and kept my head down most of the time. After getting off the bus and entering the Ames store, I paused briefly to pick up some clothes, steering clear of all the sales people wandering the aisles. Then I was ready to leave. At the checkout counter, the cashier rang up my items by casually sweeping them past an electronic scanner.

"What's your zip?" she asked.

I froze solid in horror, placed a hand on my pounding chest, and said, "What?" The cashier repeated herself, and I hesitated further in dread, as I had almost stated my old zip code from Monongahela. Then I composed myself and provided the McKeesport zip code.

Not that the zip code I muttered would have made any difference. Yet it was a commercial formality that I had never experienced before. This all the more depicts how alien the experience was for me. And I still had to navigate my way back to Tom Hose once I was finished shopping. After four consecutive years totally isolated from the outside world, I did not know how to react, let alone interact. I felt stunned.

Upon my return to that cramped bedroom after that first time out in public, I was actually relieved to be back in the locked bedroom. I almost felt safe. Much uncertainty swirled in my head about what would happen to me if I was ever discovered in the outside world. By contrast, being out in the world also had an exhilarating quality, one I couldn't deny. Nevertheless, after returning from my first excursion to Ames, my days once again became carbon copies of each other. The boredom and repetitiveness reminded me that all of the anxiety involved in getting out of that room was worth enduring.

At this point in my baffling life, my urge to move beyond the confines of that bedroom and my need for a life exceeding Thursday baths, incessant prayer, television, sex, and PlayStation inspired my dialogue with Tom Hose more and more. After many conversations where I expressed my love for him, along with my discontent for the way we were living, he promised to call a lawyer to investigate his options. In 2000, he informed me that he had contacted an attorney about our situation. Ironically, according to what Hose told me about this event, the lawyer remarked, "Wow, you could make a movie out of this story."

The advice Hose received from his attorney was impractical. For reasons I still don't understand, he was advised to move out of Pennsylvania to another state. He did not have the money to go anywhere. He paid his parents $100 a month for rent, made a weekly contribution for groceries, and gave his mother money to have her hair styled. As the health of his father declined, so did the family's finances. Money wasn't an issue for me, though. I just needed to be resilient, and most of all, I needed to get out of that bedroom whenever I could for whatever brief moments Tom Hose would permit.

I was next allowed out of the house on an afternoon in September 2000, when Eleanor and Bud were away from home. Once more, Tom Hose gave me $120.00 to go shopping for clothes. As always, he stood lookout for me as I sneaked out the back door. This time, I was not as nervous, and I navigated my way much better than I had the first time. Still, on the way home, I was anxious about spending all of the money I was given to shop. Something about that made me worry. Although my fears did not materialize into anything detrimental, I was itching to get out of the house as soon again as I could.

During this third phase of my captivity, relief came in the simplest pleasures. By this time, Tom Hose began to allow me a few other liberties. Late in the evening and after his parents were long asleep, I would quietly exit my bedroom cell, carefully descend the staircase from the second floor, and finally arrive at the back porch. Making sure to be perfectly silent, I could then enjoy the night sky and night air, hours at a time, while most of the world was off in dreams that I could only imagine. This is when I discovered the company of a feral cat, Abby. Shy and timid, she slowly warmed to me, and I placed food and milk out for her. To me, she was a gift from God to help me through the long and lonely nights that came and went in a gust of time now lost.

September 23, 2000, was Justin's seventeenth birthday. Through my conversations with Hose and him, as well as what I could pick up through the ventilation ducts in the bedroom, I knew that a convenience store, JJ's Deli Mart, was still operating at the top of Soles Street, where it intersected with Versailles Avenue, less than a city block from where we were. I begged Tom Hose to let me go to the convenience store to purchase something for Justin's birthday, and, to my surprise, he relented.

JJ's was owned and operated by Joe Sparico and his wife and daughter, Jan and Joelle. In years to come, this convenience store and those who operated it would find their fates inexplicably intertwined with mine. Yet on this occasion in September 2000, I was a complete stranger to those at JJ's.

A NEW PHASE OF CAPTIVITY

By September 2000, now that I had been twice out of the house on stealth shopping excursions, my first trip to JJ's to purchase a little something for Justin's birthday was carefully designed by his father. The people there were well-acquainted with the faces in the neighborhood. Tom Hose knew that if I ever went into JJ's, eventually, Joe would notice me as someone from outside of McKeesport.

Tom Hose was so controlling that even this small exercise of independence required him to devise a plan for me. As he did every time I was allowed out when his parents were away from home, he served as lookout. In addition, he instructed me on exactly what to say if anyone at JJ's asked me anything about myself.

"Just say you are visiting a friend and on your way home," he told me. If pressed on the identity of this friend, I was to avert the

question and just say, "Oh, just a friend on Soles Street," and leave
right away before any more questions were asked, even if I had
not completed my purchases. At this time, Hose began giving me
an allowance: ten dollars every other week.

This first trip to JJ's was exciting. I bought lots of junk food for
Justin. No one bothered me or asked any questions. I felt carefree
for a few moments and recognized how nice it was to be out on
my own, however briefly. I knew I needed more moments like this
if I was going to survive. And survival, for me, was inextricably
linked to Tom Hose with deep psychological chains that it would
take many more years for me to break. During these few and
treasured moments out on my own, I am ashamed to say that the
thought of leaving him was not an option in my mind.

For approximately the next five years, I was allowed out to
shop at Ames, Rite Aide, Foodland, or JJ's about two or three
times a year. Over time, I came to recognize Joe Sparico, the owner
of JJ's, because I would also see him coming down Soles Street
and entering the house next door as I peeked up from the bottom
of the bedroom window. Much later, I would understand why Joe
was calling upon the next door neighbor. In any event, Joe struck
me as a fatherly man, perhaps because I had nothing remotely
close to that in my life. His expressive, Italian mannerisms were
inviting. He was a kind and generous man, who often donated a
loaf of bread or a gallon of milk to customers who had no money.
Joe was also deeply protective of his family. And yes, I longed for
my father.

All of my longings and complaints to Tom Hose advanced my
liberty a bit more come Christmas 2000. As the years wore on,
Tom Hose's father became more and more ill. He had high blood
pressure and was an insulin-dependent diabetic. The number of
medications he needed to live grew, but his income was fixed
on Social Security. The costs of Bud's prescription medications
strangled the household income.

As Christmas Eve 2000 arrived, the family purchased few gifts for each other. As a result, there were fewer necessary trips up and down the steps to ferry gifts during the exchange. Tom Hose relented to closing his bedroom door so that I would not have to hide in the closet on Christmas ever again. I listened to Christmas music and savored the moment. Tom Hose got drunk. Being allowed out of the closet on Christmas Eve was a profound blessing for me but an ironic twist that the Hose family financial difficulties improved my lot in life. However, to me, this was an amazing advancement. Little things meant a lot to me then, as they do now; but make no mistake, my captivity remained, in many ways, a mental and physical hell compounded on a daily basis by a recurring and ridiculously repetitive routine. The slight deviation that allowed me out of the closet on Christmas Eve 2000 was as astonishing as it was baffling. How could I be unworthy of such a thing for so many years? How could I be so grateful for being as worthy as anyone would be to be free of such confinement? Confounded and confused, I suffered on, with Tom Hose exercising absolute control over my life.

September 11, 2001: My morning began as it always did. I woke with Tom Hose and Justin as they readied themselves and then left for the day. I turned on the television and was watching *Good Morning America,* which was showing coverage of smoke billowing from one of the two towers that comprised the World Trade Towers in New York. Then, before my very eyes, I watched in horror as I observed an airplane slam into the second tower. I began to weep, and the Hose residence buzzed with activity.

Eleanor was home, placing laundry on the line to dry, Tom Hose was at school, and Bud was in downtown McKeesport when the news of September 11 gripped the world. By this time, Justin had graduated from high school and was working at Foodland grocery store. Bud always left in the morning to get away and have coffee with friends. I heard the phone ring and overheard

Eleanor's panicked conversation with Bud. Then the neighbors began calling. I could tell each one by the nature of Eleanor's comments. With some neighbors, Eleanor had a tendency to gripe. With her classier friend, Rita, Eleanor always put on airs. Listening to Eleanor's frantic phone conversations and watching the horror on television, I was exceptionally frightened. I kept talking to myself, kept repeating, "Oh my God, Oh my God!"

I had to speak to Tom Hose. In addition to the cell phone that he carried with him, I knew that he kept in his bedroom closet an old cell phone that an ex-girlfriend had given him. I found and charged it. To my great dismay, there was no service. Obviously, the ex-girlfriend had disconnected it. I wasn't thinking clearly, and the trauma even worsened.

At some point, I heard the sound of a low-flying aircraft rip through the sky over Soles Street. Ten minutes later, the television reported that United Flight 93 had crashed in nearby Shanksville, Pennsylvania. I am convinced that United Flight 93 was the horrible noise I heard overhead. It broke my heart, and I wondered about my parents at that moment. Although I am not sure why, I felt incredible fear that my mother and father were on one of the planes.

As September 11, 2001 wore on at Cornell, an early dismissal of students was declared, and parents began to pick their children up from school. My worst worry as I watched the towers smolder was that they would collapse. Then I watched in dismay as they fell. I was only thankful that I never saw any of the people who jumped from the towers prior to their collapse. Somehow, I was spared the sight of those televised images for the better, as I remember the same desire to jump out of Tom Hose's bedroom window almost overcame me in the helplessness of my seclusion there.

He returned home from work early. I was emotionally exhausted, scared, and a feeling of helplessness consumed me. As he entered the room, I fell into his arms and began sobbing uncontrollably. He held me, and for once, he did not yell at me for crying. He, too, was upset about what had happened that day, but I never once saw him cry about that or anything.

THE ALIAS: NIKKI DIANE ALLEN

About a year later, I knew Tom Hose was watching me in a different way than he had before. I could not hide my growing need to escape my prison, even though I knew doing so was next to impossible.

"What's wrong?" he asked me time and again.

And time and again, I said, "Please consult that lawyer you saw before. Maybe he can find a way for..."

For what? For Tom Hose to miraculously transform from captor to Prince Charming? For him to be able to set me free without going to jail for keeping me captive? I didn't know. I only felt that he needed to get a legal opinion.

"Okay," he told me one day. "I made an appointment to see him."

Maybe my time had finally come. I couldn't think about anything else until he returned.

"Well," he told me once he was home and back in his room, "the attorney hadn't expected me to come back. He said he was surprised that we're still together."

"Really?"

I suspected, of course, that he had grown as tired of our situation as I had and that his lawyer must have gleaned this from their first consultation.

"He repeated what he told me the first time. Nothing new."

Although this upset me, I felt stuck and could not imagine anything I could do to escape my situation. Regardless of those moments when he allowed me certain controlled outlets, such as to let me shop for personal items at Ames, RiteAide, Foodland, or JJ's, or to enjoy late evenings on the back porch, my captivity lingered on over many more years. The monotony and wearisome resemblance of each day to the next was becoming impossible.

During this time, in some ways, I tried to exercise a modicum of control over my life. Although I had quit smoking early on, I started again in 2003. While I could have purchased cigarettes for myself during my occasional ventures out of the house, instead, I simply smoked down the cigarette butts Tom Hose left in the bedroom ashtray. Though it seems odd and slight, psychologists later suggested that this was a means by which I was attempting to gain some control over my situation. I had no idea that in less than two years, I would arrive at a path to my salvation. Time moved incredibly slowly, and I was often dispirited and detached from the almost-exact sameness that each day of my life portrayed. Although my memory becomes blurry amidst the repetitiveness, some things stand out in the fog as if painted in my mind.

What stands out most in these years that comprise my third period of captivity were the attempts that Tom Hose made to elevate my spirits one way or another. He began purchasing Avon products for me after I turned eighteen. Oddly enough, he placed the orders through a teacher at Cornell, where everyone now knew that he had a girlfriend. I loved shopping through the Avon catalogue because I had greater luxury of time and no worries about being discovered in public, as opposed to those times when I hurried out and back to the house on rare and secret shopping excursions.

Just before Christmas 2004, and then again on Christmas Eve 2004, Tom Hose put forth his strongest effort to keep me content in my growing unhappiness. By this time, Bud had so many medical problems that he and Eleanor were traveling and leaving the house much less. This meant less liberty for me as well. I would get my hopes up when I learned that Bud and Eleanor were planning to go out, only to have those hopes dashed when they would cancel their plans. I grew more and more gravely lonely, and many years in seclusion left me frustrated and angry.

Tom Hose knew that, and on November 4, 2004, he asked me to marry him. I accepted. Then, on the following Christmas Eve, he gave me a card in which he wrote down this proposal. I again said yes and wrote my acceptance in the card.

He then began telling me false tales of his trips to jewelry stores in the mall, where he was shopping for just the perfect engagement ring. What's strange to me now is that I really would have married him back in 2004. Prior to the last period of my captivity, the last ten months, when I assumed an alias and began quasi-regular interaction with the world at large, I still believed that I loved him. Up to this time, I would have defended him as the only person in the world who cared for me. Despite all I suffered, I had no idea my relationship with Tom Hose was as strange as it was until I had the opportunity to see what normal relationships were like. Aside from the relationship between my paternal grandparents, which I could barely remember from so far back before my captivity, I had known no such thing as a truly loving relationship between any man and woman in my life, certainly not as it pertained to my father and Jo-Ann—especially not as it pertained to my father and mother. At twenty-two years old, after years of psychological torture and sexual degradation, I was, in fact, prepared to marry Tom Hose. Thankfully, that would change.

In April 2005, the worst possible thing happened for the better. Up to that time, after unceremoniously graduating from high school, Justin worked normal hours, as if he had been in school, and his schedule did not really affect me. I still had the afternoons to myself with Justin and his father away at work. In April 2005, however, Justin changed jobs and began working at Wal-Mart on the night shift. Life for me got really tough after that. Justin would sleep in the room all day, so I no longer had the room to myself. Even with earphones, I could not listen to the radio or watch the television. I had to be more silent than ever so as not to wake Justin, who was lying there sleeping next to the bed I shared with his father.

As Bud's medical condition worsened, he virtually became a shut-in and never left the house, further impinging on the few moments when I was able to enjoy some autonomy in my weird captivity.

Tom Hose went from proposing marriage to absolute apathy about our relationship. He complained about the smell from the bucket of my waste that he had to empty each day and forced me to cover it with one of my shirts before he would remove it. He even became inattentive to my needs and would fail to leave toilet paper for me. I resorted to using paper from my notebook and was so down and upset that I began to contemplate suicide. My spiritual beliefs would not allow that escape, yet I strongly questioned for what possible purpose God had left me on Earth. I prayed for Him to take me and end my miserable existence.

But I did far more than just pray. That was when I really started to bitch about it. I complained to Tom Hose; I begged. I even threatened. Once silent, I could now no longer shut my mouth about how I must—and would—escape the prison of the bedroom.

Looking back, I am glad that Justin's hours, Bud's illness, and Tom Hose's treatment of me forced me to demand something more in my life. A few months later, I found it in my alias, Nikki Diane Allen. My salvation was drawing near.

LIFE AS SOMEONE ELSE

I obtained my alias, Nikki Diane Allen, haphazardly but with some basis in the life I had lost nine years earlier.

"We'll call you Nikki," Tom Hose said, "since your middle name's Nicole."

"Why can't I just be Nicole then?" I asked.

"No," he said. "Your name will be Nikki."

Dian is my mother's middle name, so I made that my assumed middle name, although I did not know any better and spelled it wrong by adding the letter "e" at the end.

"What do you think about Diane?" I asked him. "Do you suppose anyone will suspect?"

"Suspect what?" he said. "Nobody cares about your middle name, Tanya. Nobody cares, period. If they did..."

I didn't need any reminders.

Instead of arguing with him, I opened a phone book and blindly pointed my finger to a name.

"Allen," I said, and my voice trembled. "I am Nicole Diane Allen."

"Nikki," he corrected me.

"Right. Nikki Diane Allen."

I almost felt like that other person.

Then, as with just about everything else in my world, fortune allowed me an opportunity to begin an assumed life. In June 2005, Bud Hose experienced a broken blood vessel in one of his legs and was hospitalized. He suffered a prolonged stay in the hospital because his ailments made it difficult for him to walk. As he prepared to leave the hospital, he knew he needed assistance at home. Tom Hose and I both realized the opportunity presented by this situation.

From early on, upon realizing that his father would be hospitalized for a prolonged period, Tom Hose mentioned to his parents that he had a girlfriend. Then, while his father remained in the hospital, he made sure his father knew that his girlfriend, now called Nikki, was coming by daily and helping out. Eleanor Hose went to the hospital every day and dutifully relayed messages about their son's new girlfriend to Bud.

As I realized from the beginning, Tom Hose controlled his mother more than anyone. That is how he managed to go virtually all his life without a job before he began working for St. Moritz Security Company. Once he moved back with his parents after his failed marriage, his family just could not support him and Justin on their fixed income. That was when his mother stood up to him for possibly the only time in her life and made him get a job. But she only pushed him that hard out of necessity. In all other ways she remained her son's pawn and even more so in the midst of Bud's medical crisis.

Tom Hose unleashed an unrelenting barrage on his mother in favor of "Nikki coming to live with us" to help out with all of Bud's needs when he returned home from the hospital.

The fact that Tom Hose and his father despised each other should have made Bud wonder about his son's offer to help. The two would avoid each other at all cost, and long before I ever lived there, Tom Hose maintained a great distance from his father by shutting himself off in his bedroom whenever he could. This pathetic relationship between father and son made the closed and virtually unknown existence that Tom Hose and I achieved in that bedroom all the more understandable.

In fact, Bud and Eleanor came to fear their son from an early age. On one occasion, long before I was relegated to listening from the vents of his closet, Eleanor found marijuana in Hose's bedroom and confiscated it. He confronted his mother and told her he knew that she must have taken his stash. He threatened his mother and told her that he was going out for an hour, and when he came back, she better have returned the weed to where she found it or he would "burn this fucking house down." Petrified, Eleanor returned the marijuana and relinquished her authority over the criminal activities of her son.

On another occasion, when Tom Hose was just thirteen, he kicked his father in the groin after his father attempted to punish him for some teenage misbehavior. Expelled from the private Catholic school where his parents enrolled him (he was always skipping school as a child) and having never graduated from high school, he exhibited the worse qualities as a kid, such as bullying and stealing, to name a few. He was entirely undisciplined as a child, and he acted as he wanted. His parents could not control him. In fact, he even boasted that his parents were scared to death of him.

Given their bad relationship with their son, even Eleanor should have been more suspicious when Hose decided to introduce me to them as his girlfriend who needed a place to live and who could help Bud out around the house.

Bud and Eleanor were not too smart.

I was eaten up with nerves the first time I was to meet them face-to-face on the day Eleanor came home from the hospital with Bud. Pacing back and forth in the Hose family living room, I awaited the arrival of two people I had strangely known for nine years and only by the sounds of their voices through a ventilation duct or the walls of the room where I had been held captive. At some point, my pacing was so intense that Justin finally barked, "Sit the fuck down."

As Eleanor and Bud Hose entered their house and encountered me for the first time, the introduction was remarkably unremarkable. Both Eleanor and Bud greeted me politely, and we exchanged some pleasantries. After hearing their movements and voices all of those years, I expected that both Eleanor and Bud would be overweight, as they were. However, the scowl on Eleanor's face was a surprise to me, and I had not expected that Bud would be so homely. When I had the misfortune to finally meet Tom Hose's mother, I thought that if he dressed in drag, he would look exactly like a taller, thinner version of her.

After the introductions were out of the way, I walked over to some of my things that I had placed in the living room as part of this ruse, gathered them, and walked up the stairs to the bedroom where I had been hidden for more than nine years, just as if I had never been up there all that time. In an instant, I was quasi-liberated to the very place of my captivity in yet another situation where the truth was always more peculiar than fiction. Still, after nine years of a stilted existence in that room, psychologically tortured and sexually degraded, I was hardly free in any traditional sense of the word.

Tom Hose came up and hugged me, calmed me, and encouraged me that it all went well.

The fourth and final phase of my captivity began on June 17, 2005, as I began using the assumed name of Nikki Diane Allen. True to Tom Hose's scheming and domineering character, after I assumed my alias and was introduced to Bud and Eleanor, he still kept a tight rein on my coming and going when he was able. But when he would leave for work, I was exposed, literally, to a whole new world, especially as that world pertained to Eleanor Hose.

In the beginning of these last ten months of life in the Hose residence, Eleanor and I were friendly. We would shop for groceries together on Saturdays. Even such a humdrum event as grocery shopping was amazing to me, as I had not been to a grocery store in more than four years. The last time was on one of those clandestine occasions when Tom Hose let me out of the house to purchase something from Foodland, so I did not have the luxury of time to check out the cornucopia of new and different products in the grocery store.

Now I lingered at Foodland, taking in every vegetable, every meat, every new product as if admiring art in a museum. My amazement must have been odd to Eleanor. Not long after that, our relationship soured. There were many reasons why we began to dislike each other.

Aside from my odd behavior in the grocery store, I was, in certain ways, stunted in my social development from the age of fourteen onward. Eleanor was skeptical about a young and strange girl (me) dating her son. Furthermore, my obsession with my physical appearance also struck Eleanor as superficial, shallow, and irritating. I probably did seem weird to her; I had forgotten how to interact with a stranger—even a stranger whose life I had been overhearing for years through walls and floorboards.

And my obsession with my appearance was one of the few ways I could hold onto what was left of my self-esteem.

My oddities aside, until the time I met Bud and Eleanor, I understood their relationship solely from the twisted accounts provided by their son, as well as staccato bursts of conversation I heard from time to time while I was trapped in their son's bedroom. In full view of the relationship between Eleanor and Bud, despite how much I grew to dislike her, I recognized that Bud had a compassionate and caring love for his wife.

I even grew somewhat fond of Bud. Unlike his son, he was a genuinely nice guy. To see the relationship between him and Eleanor firsthand opened my eyes about my absurd relationship with their son. Over the next ten months, as I began to observe many different relationships among loving people, I began to recognize my relationship with Tom Hose as entirely abnormal. Yet it would take all the courage I could muster to seize my freedom from him.

THE PATH TO EMANCIPATION

My father's second wife, Jo-Anne McGuire, once described me as "streetwise" as she tried to claim a part in the media frenzy that shortly followed my release in March 2006. Indeed, my path to my ten-year perdition with Tom Hose began on the streets of McKeesport. But my road to independence rose up out of a church.

It was a blazing-hot summer day in July 2005. Eleanor had become demeaning and offensive. When I offered to do some ironing, Eleanor said, "You don't know how to iron."

"How do you know?" I asked.

That beady-eyed glare of contempt came again. "Yeah, right, you? Ms. Priss, give me a break."

When I tried to vacuum the carpet or dust the furniture, Eleanor said, "Let me do it. You don't want to mess up your hair or makeup."

Tom Hose and I discussed the situation between his mother and me, and he decided to have a conversation with her about it. I decided to leave the house for a while so they could speak in private.

As I walked the streets of McKeesport that scorching summer day, drenched in sweat, I came upon a sign at the Beulah Park United Methodist Church. Growing up, my parents were Methodist, so the thrift store sign at Beulah Park United Methodist Church appealed to me on that sentimental and spiritual level. The church thrift store was open, and I went in for a look around and to cool off.

The people in the thrift store were very nice. They greeted me and asked if they could offer me any help. When I had left the house that day, I had no idea that I would find my way into a church thrift store and suddenly felt self-conscious about my appearance.

"I'm sorry," I said, looking down at my short shorts. "I know it's disrespectful to be dressed this way in a thrift store associated with the church, but I didn't know I'd be coming here."

"Don't worry," said a smiling woman, and the others nodded agreement. "I'm Jennifer. You're welcome here."

Soon, I found myself talking about my Methodist faith with Jennifer. I enjoyed my first visit there so much that I returned several times over the next four weeks. On one of those trips, I noticed that Jennifer needed help moving a table, and I offered to help.

"Thanks," she said. "You've been here before, haven't you? You wore shorts the first time and were all worried."

I nodded. "I told you that I'm a Methodist."

"That's right." She paused, as if trying to make her mind up about something or maybe just about me. "Nikki, would you be interested in helping out on a regular basis?"

Nikki? Daily basis? Me?

I swallowed hard and said, "I'd love to."

Just like that, I was working in the clothing room of the thrift store and becoming involved with the Beulah Park Methodist Church. It was not long before I began attending church services and Bible study. The first time, I felt ashamed. I remembered many years ago in Bible camp pledging not to have sex before marriage. And I knew that I had been living in sin all of these years. Ultimately, I came to terms with all of this and with God. I knew I had been drawn to church, as many sinners are drawn, and my faith renewed in earnest.

Tom Hose, on the other hand, hated the idea of my worshiping outside the Roman Catholic Church that his family attended. Fast losing control over me, he had no choice except to relent and pretend to encourage me to attend the church I had found. He even arranged for Joyce Brown, the secretary at Cornell, who also attended Beulah Park United Methodist Church, to drive me there on Sundays. Amazingly, Joyce Brown was also the secretary at Cornell when I attended that school in 1995 and 1996. Later, she claimed she didn't recognize me.

I know that God put me into that thrift store, and since then, my spirituality received a long-awaited nurturing. I grew stronger in prayer as I increasingly realized freedom from my captor. I understood that it would be darkest before the dawn, but an awakening was forthcoming, and Tom Hose probably saw this.

He continually bristled at my choice of a Methodist Church and my relationship with his mother, and he decided to cut me off from the ten-dollar allowance he had previously been giving me. This was another bad decision on his part, as it drove me further from his control.

After that, I struggled for ways to make money, and I frequently complained about my situation to Joe Sparico, the owner of JJ's, who tried to get me a job. He had no way of knowing that I could not work any legitimate job, since I had no idea what my social security number was or if I even had one. I had no choice but to become evasive with Joe, which only added to his doubts and a sense that something was not right with this girl who did not have any documentation as to her identity.

I came to know Joe and Jan Sparico as two tough products of McKeesport, and they would need their strength for that which awaited them with me. Jan was a Vietnam-era veteran of the United States Air Force. Joe was a native of McKeesport and a former car salesman. He would not hesitate to tell you, "I've been jammed up with the law" on occasion for past illegal gambling with poker machines in his convenience store, JJ's Deli Mart. The Sparicos's daughter, Joelle, helped out working at the convenience store from time to time. Her only sibling, brother Shaun, was a former McKeesport cop who did not need to work at JJ's. He stayed clean in the force and got out early. Joe and Jan had been married for nearly fifty years and were both in their late sixties. They had also operated another store nearby before that. They were blind to the hidden cause of my problems. Their frustration with me was mounting.

In any event, as my financial hardship mounted, I was tempted with illegal gambling. I was aware of a woman in the neighborhood who booked numbers for, among others, Tom Hose and his mother, Eleanor. Not everyone realizes what is involved with being a bookie, but I recognized this practice because of them. Both mother and son had a favorite number, and they would send "Nikki" to the bookie to play each week.

This underground system works off of the officially sanctioned state lottery daily-number games. Each day, the state lottery sells tickets for, and draws winning numbers from, its lottery system. Bookies take bets and money from individuals who want to gamble on the numbers that will be drawn. If a person bets on a number that is drawn, the bookie pays out just like the state lottery would have paid, but with two important exceptions. First, no tax is withheld from the payout, nor is any presumably paid to the state by the winner. Second, the bookie will take smaller bets than the state. Big bets are laid off between bookies to reduce risk on a big payout, and many bookies employ several workers to help them take calls, record bets, and handle the business.

The Soles Street neighborhood bookie allowed me to hang around while the whole numbers operation buzzed on. I liked being there. It was time away from the Hose residence and "girl time" because there were three women running the show that I really liked, especially Margie. She was a good listener, and she let me style her hair. Working with these tough, kind women made me feel important.

Booking was not the only illegal avenue open to me for making money. I could have done far worse, as McKeesport offered plentiful opportunities in drug dealing, nude dancing, or prostitution, but I never engaged in these activities due to my spirituality. I would have rather lived under a bridge than sell my body or harm anyone with drugs. By contrast, I did not see booking as harmful to anyone. Unfortunately, I did not excel with numbers or math. So, as much as the bookies enjoyed my company, I was not cut out for the job. Still, I found a means to make some money for a couple of months, from November 2005 into January 2006. Regardless of the means by which I survived my terrible ordeal, my captivity with Tom Hose was drawing to an end.

As he had lost a substantial measure of control over me after he allowed me to assume my identity as Nikki, he remained a control freak in ways that were just intolerable. Despite the fact that I may have had relative freedom once I assumed my alias, my liberty remained restricted to those times while Tom Hose was working at Cornell. I had to make sure that I was home inside the Soles Street residence by the time he returned from work at 3:30. I was mostly penniless. I began to pray for the strength to leave.

The way out was emerging to me as I had befriended the owner of JJ's, Joe Sparico, as well as my bookie neighbor, Margie, and many from my church. As a result, I was realizing from the example of those in normal relationships that my relationship with Tom Hose was anything but normal. Here, too, I could see that these relationships were not at all controlling in any way, whereas Tom Hose controlled virtually every facet of my life. Still, he had provided for me all of those years when I thought that no one cared about me. My alias was a way in which he seemed to be trying against his better judgment to accommodate my need for an identity and some form of life at large. These contradictions caused me to contemplate my future without Tom Hose.

Once I could no longer see my way to a future with Tom Hose, anger began to rise in me. While I reconciled all that was involved with leaving, I had no idea where I would go. I feared retribution from Tom Hose, and leaving simply presented me with a vast, unknown world.

Anger should never control your choices. I decided to endure one more Christmas with him. Just one more. And then I promised myself that I would escape for good.

A FINAL CHRISTMAS IN CAPTIVITY

Christmas 2005 as Nikki Allen was much better than all of the other ones had been. A few days before, I took a bus to Walmart and purchased butter, flower, sugar, ribbons, bows, and just about everything I needed to bake and wrap Christmas cookies. The packages were heavy, and I had to walk up a steep hill in the snow to carry them home, but I did not mind. I made banana, chocolate chip (with and without walnuts), and oatmeal-raisin cookies. I also purchased decorative tins from my church thrift shop and packaged gifts for those I cared about. I gave cookie tins to all the girls at the thrift shop, as well as the Sparicos and others with whom I had now become acquainted. I loved being able to purchase Christmas cards for the bookies, the women at the church thrift store, and a manicurist I had come to know. What many might have taken for granted as a simple token of giving in a seasonal spirit was an outright miracle for me. I respected the holiday with a reverence and enthusiasm matched by few.

When I think about the prior holidays with Tom Hose, it's as if another person cowered in that upstairs closet. And in many ways, I was another person. At that time, Tom Hose had convinced me that he was the only one who cared about me and that I would be homeless or dead if I ever disobeyed him. He was so masterful in his control techniques that, even when circumstances might have convinced me otherwise, he manipulated those circumstances to serve his end. Thank God that Tom Hose was nearing the end of his manipulation of my life, but that didn't stop him from continuously attempting to control me.

Although I spent Christmas Eve dinner 2005 with Tom Hose and his family, it was only because he insisted. I was not getting along with him or his mother, and I wanted to be with Margie, the bookie. On Christmas, he called me at Margie's house and demanded that I return for dinner with his family. The following day, I went to the Beulah Park Methodist Church, and the Hose family went to Catholic Church.

Soon after Christmas 2005, I realized I was enjoying a better quality of life under my assumed identity. Karen manicured my nails, and I was regularly spending time during the day with Joe Sparico or Margie. Although I loved my work at the thrift store, I was sick of the rule that had me back in that house by the time Tom Hose came home from work every day. I needed a better life. I craved it.

One day, while I was at JJ's visiting with Joe Sparico, I found myself feeling uncomfortable when a man I did not immediately recognize was staring intensely at me. I was about to say something to the middle-aged man who was leering at me when both the man and I caught a light of recognition in each other's eyes.

The man was E. Michael Elias. I am certain that this former McKeesport juvenile lieutenant, with whom I had interacted on past runaway experiences more than a decade before, and who was initially assigned to investigate my disappearance ten years before, had recognized me, just as I had recognized him.

I thought that Elias had the power to break my alias and expose my past ten years with Tom Hose. Maybe it was just a matter of time before this nightmare would come to an end. Not that day, apparently. Elias quickly shot out of JJ's.

I went home and excitedly told Tom Hose about the incident at JJ's, but he wasn't impressed.

"Probably just some perverted old man staring at a pretty young girl," he said.

What irony that a perverted old man like Tom Hose would reach such a conclusion. I felt otherwise, but this feeling alone was not by itself responsible for my ultimate decision to wrest myself from the control of Hose.

It was late in March of 2006, and I had been without any source of money since the beginning of the year. The summer was fast approaching, and I was dreading that the Hose residence would become a searing misery in the summer, with only the box fans for the windows. Although I was nearly ready to leave, I worried that without my true identity, I would have no legal way of providing for myself.

I prayed with all my might. Nearly every Sunday for ten months, I was at church, praying for guidance in my situation. Finally, as I summoned the courage to do something about my situation, fearing all the while for my life, I found strength in, of all places, the horoscopes printed in the *McKeesport Daily News*. Reading my horoscope for that day, I considered telling Joe my true identity. I saw these words: "You will be thinking big thoughts and getting more firmly in touch with your own destiny. Decisions come swiftly." As if that was not concurrence enough, Tom Hose's horoscope for the same day read: "You're very likely going to discover just what you are made of and how you compare, favorably, or unfavorably, to the competition."

I needed to read Joe Sparico's horoscope. The coincidence seemed uncanny to one who had come to know Joe as well as I did: "You're spending too much energy safeguarding your reputation. Trust in those around you. They'll give you your due." Somehow these prophecies were a final indication to me that I could wait no longer to risk my life and escape Tom Hose. Yes, I was frightened, but I was ready to take a hold of my future.

At the same time, my loitering at JJ's began to wear on Joe. He did not understand my situation, and he was nearing his wits' end trying to help me without success. Finally, Joe snapped:

I told her, "Why do you put up with that crap, why don't you just leave … ?" I was sort of mad, because she was putting up with this crap, you know. She was just antsy and fidgety and, you know, I don't know if she cried then or not, but, you know … all along, throughout her coming up to my place, it was always, you know, me and my wife and my daughter, always telling her, "Get away from him, leave him, why do you stick with him?" You know. Unbeknownst to us that she couldn't very well leave, because she had nowhere else to go, you know. And I think she told me, she said, "I really don't have nowhere to go." And I said, "Gee, there's women's shelters, there's a place like that for you to go. Why don't you go there or something?" you know … We couldn't understand why. Until after the fact.

I left JJ's that day very upset.

The next morning, I returned to JJ's. I sensed that Joe remained angry and frustrated with me. I went into a back room to play the video poker machines. Joe kept coming in and out of the room in between waiting on customers. When Joe was in the back room with me, he began smacking various buttons on the poker machines and grousing about my situation. Joe kept saying, "Something is just not right here." That's when I began shaking uncontrollably. I started to cry.

Joe asked me, "Why are you crying?"

I responded, "Do you care about me?"

"Of course," Joe replied. "When I think of you, I think of my daughter."

A long period ensued where I kept crying and shaking, and Joe kept asking me what was wrong. Finally, I whispered to Joe, "There is something I need to tell you. I am not who you think I am. I did a horrible thing. I screwed up my life horribly."

That's when Joe asked me if I robbed somebody.

"No," I responded.

So, Joe asked, "Did you kill somebody?"

Again, I said, "No."

After the pause that followed, my world would change forever.

RESCUED

"My real name is Tanya Nicole Kach."

I had actually done it; I had trusted another person. I moved close up in front of Joe's face, the way I did when I spoke to others, pleading to be recognized.

"Okay." Joe stepped back. "Then what are you doing here? Why the pretending?"

Although I could hear the doubt in his voice, I knew it was time to tell the truth. My parents' names. My abduction. Everything.

Joe listened patiently but skeptically. Another long silence passed between us. Then, without saying another word, Joe turned toward me and told me to go about my business normally. "Don't do anything out of the ordinary. I'll take care of everything." "You need to go back there, to that house," he told me. "One more time. Don't let on what's happening. Just act normal until the police get there."

"Police?" It was really happening. I couldn't stop it now.

Then he told me to call him later.

Meanwhile, he called the National Center for Missing and Exploited Children. To his shock—and mine—they confirmed my status. He then called the McKeesport Police, who, true to their indifferent ways, asked if he could call back the next day because they were busy. Joe was astounded, but he contacted his son, Shaun, a former McKeesport cop, who remembered my case from during his days on the force ten years before. Shaun used his contacts to spur the police into action.

The doors were about to be blown off my life. When I revealed my true identity to Joe, I had few ideas about what would happen next. Maybe we would talk about what I should do, the way fathers and daughters talked over things. Maybe days, weeks, possibly even months later, I would be able to somehow have a normal life. In short, I was not prepared for the swift and dramatic reaction by Joe and others when they learned who I really was.

Stunned and uncertain about what would happen next, I did what I was told. I left to run errands. It was as if nothing happened. I trusted Joe. Still, it was strange that nothing seemed to be happening in light of my confession to Joe. Late that Tuesday afternoon, I returned to the Soles Street home where I had been captive for more than ten years. *Will I really be able to do this? Was Joe telling the truth? Please, God, let me get out of here.*

I walked into the shabby living room. *Never again. Please. Never again.*

Eleanor was busying herself around the house. I knew Bud and Justin were upstairs sleeping. Tom Hose was reading the newspaper and drinking tea from the pitcher on the counter. If I could keep away from him, I might be able to go through with this, but there was no turning back.

My nerves fraying by the moment, I waited in the kitchen, stared out of the window, and watched for whatever was to come. As I waited, I slipped away into the basement to use a prepaid cell phone to call Joe for updates on my situation.

At first, when Joe answered his phone, I did not know how to identify myself. *Should I say, "It's Nikki?" Or should I say, "It's Tanya?"* I stuttered and said, "It's me." He recognized the sound of my voice and told me that he had contacted the police.

"…As a matter of fact, the police just walked into my store. Try and call me back in fifteen minutes."

After I returned to the kitchen, Tom Hose came downstairs to refill his empty tea glass. Ten years of complacency, domination, and deviance seemed as if they defined the contours of his winced face. His faux-black hair, badly in need of a trim, added to his odd appearance, as if he were an evil character from a comic strip. The security uniform he wore made him look even more ludicrous.

"What you doing, kitty?" he asked, as he had at least a thousand times before.

I almost told him, but as I stared at the drawer of knives within his reach, I said nothing.

He left the kitchen and went back upstairs to his room. I then sneaked down into the basement and called Joe again.

"It's me again," I said when he answered the phone.

"They're on their way right now," he said.

Oh my God!

I went back upstairs to the kitchen. Eleanor Hose entered to make dinner.

"Are you going to make the pancakes tonight?" she asked in a sarcastic voice.

"No," I said. "No, I'm not."

"But you're going to eat the pancakes, aren't you?" She glared at me with beady, black eyes.

"No."

I shouldn't have said that. What if Tom Hose had heard me? He'd demand to know what I meant, and I wouldn't have answers.

I fled the kitchen to get away from Eleanor and sat in the living room, so nervous about not knowing what would come next.

Moments later, through the living room window, I saw a McKeesport cop that I recognized from the streets step up onto the front porch. I jumped out of the chair and opened the door.

The officer looked me straight in the face. "Are you Tanya Nicole Kach?" he asked.

"Yes."

Other officers surrounded the house.

"Where is he?" the cop asked.

I pointed above my head to the second floor. "Upstairs. He has no idea."

The cop asked, "Does he have any weapons?"

"No," I said.

Three officers went up, guns drawn. Relaxing in his room, Tom Hose had been playing dumb when the police entered. While compliant with the officers' directions, he demanded to know what was going on. They brought Tom Hose downstairs.

"Sit," one of them said and pointed at a chair. "And shut up."

His face was a conflicting expression of confusion and anger.

"What's going on?" he asked me. "Please, tell me. What's going on?"

I turned to him and said, "It's over."

He looked back at me, his face now red and full of rage.

Eleanor entered the room again.

"Why are you in my house?" She was trembling and animated, her arms raised above her head.

"Do you see this young lady here?" the lead officer asked. "Your son has been holding her in this house for over ten years, since she was fourteen years old. Your son is going to be under arrest."

Except for her ever-present scowl, Eleanor was stone faced.

"Okay." With that, she walked back into the kitchen, sat down, and stared out of the window.

"Grab some garbage bags," the officer told me. "Get your stuff. I'll escort you."

Was I really doing this? I must be, because my feet went up those stairs and into the bedroom. I crawled over the bed to the side of the room where my belongings sat.

"Wake up," I called to Justin. "It's over."

After I filled a garbage bag with my possessions, the police officer and I went back downstairs, and I grabbed another bag for some remaining clothes. Then I went back up the stairs—this time without a police escort.

Justin was awake and standing in the doorway to the bedroom. The look on his face was so menacing that I feared he might hit me.

"You told Joe," he said. "Didn't you?"

I stared into his eyes. "Yeah, I did."

Justin stepped aside. Although I was scared, I blew right past him into the bedroom and gathered up the rest of my possessions as Justin just stood there and watched. Turning around to view the dungeon of a bedroom one last time, I then walked down the stairs and out of a nightmare.

"Can I say something to her?" Tom Hose begged the police officers.

"Shut up," the lead officer replied.

When I was almost out the front door, Hose shouted, "Judas!"

Years and years of a miserable existence ended in an instant. Tom Hose glared at me with contempt, a fierce look consuming his angry face, as I walked out of that Soles Street hell house forever.

My mind was racing. Where was I going? What would life be like from here? What was God's plan for me now? I had no idea where I would go. For some crazy reason, I remembered Tom Hose telling me that when his ex-wife left him for another man, she left with only the shirt on her back. And he also told me that he threw all of her clothes and belongings in the trash. I figured I would never again see anything I left behind, yet the police officers hastened me along. By this time I had three cats.

I regretted leaving behind the cats but feared being homeless out in the streets. *My God,* I thought, *I'm about to be out on the street. I can't do that to my cats.* So I left the cats behind. With so much that had occurred over the past ten years, I was not thinking clearly at all.

I was taken for a lengthy police interview by the McKeesport Police. At first, I was placed in a small, windowless office with "Wanted" and "Missing" posters covering the walls. Although I searched for any pictures of me, I didn't find any. The room had a desk, two chairs, and a filing cabinet. After a while, I was moved to a larger room with several desks and a dry-erase chalkboard. The police provided me with a cup of water and an ashtray. I must have smoked a whole pack of cigars as I gave a statement to several police officers.

When I was fourteen-years-old, I ran away to my uncle's and aunt's in 1996. My uncle wanted to have sex with me that night. I kindly turned him down, no sex took place, then I went home and ran away again to Tom Hose. He said he would take care of me, no worries. And so for the past ten years, I've been living with him in a little bedroom in a little house. I went to the bathroom in a bucket. Showered only a couple of times a week, but he did take care of me financially. Ten months ago he let me 'so called' move in (so his parents thought), but I can't go back to school or get a real job. I wanted to leave, but felt threatened. There are times he warned me what would happen if I did leave. Played mind games, saying where would you go? So I thought I'd be on the streets, but I met Joe Sparico and the Sparico family. And today, on March 21 I told Joe. I trust him very much. Tom also made

me change my name to Nikki Allen. I just want to be
who I am, Tanya Nicole Kach"

I don't even remember how I formed the thoughts by which my
horrible path was boiled down to a paragraph. Other than some
punctuation, the statement is exactly as written. I was certainly in
shock at the time, but the statement fairly sums up that moment
in time, absent of the depth of abuse I suffered.

After I finished writing it, the police returned me to my
father, who, somewhat to his credit, had marked every day since
I'd disappeared ten years, one month, and eleven days prior. Just
as his attempts to initiate dependency proceedings for me back
in 1996 had seemed more so directed at my mom than at me, my
father's watchfulness over the years of my disappearance seemed
more so intended for the police than for me. In fact, the police
had interviewed him again back near the time when I would have
turned eighteen to follow up and see if I had made any contact
with him. Although he had not heard from me in all of those years,
he expressed an intention to have me reported as "Not missing"
so that he " ... would not have to worry about her anymore."

Gene Riazi, the officer who questioned him at that time, told
him that my case would always remain open until I was found,
either dead or alive, but that he feared the worst.

According to Riazi, my father seemed indifferent to these
comments, so I'm guessing that he marked each day of my
disappearance because he felt some obligation to prove to the
police that he somehow cared about me in this regard. Even if he
truly marked the days with the heartache that most fathers would
feel, he subsequently revealed himself as numb when it came to
his feelings for me once I was returned to him. But it would take
some time before I could sort this out.

Also, Riazi spoke with Judy and I learned that Judy had come
to warn Hose that the police had questioned her, and that she had

given them his name. I was discovering much about the way that others behaved during my captivity.

In one way or another, after my rescue, Hose admitted many of the astounding facts revealed in this book, but he could not bring himself to recognize them for what they were. For instance, although he acknowledged that my mom called him about the phone bill not long after I began my isolation in his bedroom, he claimed that I was free to yell out if I wanted. Likewise, he admitted that he might have told me all I remember him saying, such as pointing out when my mother remarried or stating that I was nothing without him, but he admitted no motives for his actions. Although he denied that he ever threatened my life, he admitted that there were times when I wanted to leave and even packed my things to go. In these instances, he made the ridiculous and absurd claim that he and I " ... talked it out."

One question presented to Tom Hose during a deposition that was conducted after my rescue says it all:

Q: Prior to Ms. Kach obtaining her alias ... from February 1996 until June 2005 ... in your mind, did she ever disobey you, once ever?

A: Not that I can recall.

Still, all that mattered was my new freedom and the fact that I was delighted to be reunited with family. My first thoughts were, *I can't believe I'm free.* Probably the next thing that happened foreshadowed tough times for my father and me in the future, because he had to contact my mom and inform her of my return. His deep-seated hatred for her began to percolate to the surface of his otherwise emotionless state of being, even though she and I were reunited a few days later. How could he be happy to see me, yet not want her to? I still had a lot to figure out and many unanswered questions to consider.

The next day, Hose surrendered and was charged with child sex offenses, corrupting the morals of a minor, and interfering with the custody of a minor. His attorney, Jim Ecker, known for defending the worst of the mostly guilty during his lengthy career, supervised an interview between Hose and the police. Ecker stated that his client would only give a statement regarding me from the period of 2005 to the present. Hose then stated that he had introduced me to his parents after his father had returned home from a hospital stay in June 2005. He offered little else beyond acknowledging his duties at Cornell and confirming that, since his separation and divorce from his ex-wife, he'd had no sexual relationships with any "adult."

Following the interview, authorities executed a search warrant for Hose's second-floor bedroom. There they seized three paper bags containing assorted homemade greeting cards I'd created and given to Hose memorializing the occasions that passed as he kept me in that room all of those years. Other sundry items included a few photos of me taken in the bedroom, as well as one of a vibrator. Finally, there were thirty-one date/calendar books that Hose made me keep over the years. He had me record our sexual encounters so he could brag to friends about his sex life. The date/calendar books record my orgasms and his orgasms, as well as what type of sex we had. I used a color code: blue for oral sex, yellow for vaginal sex, and a star for anal sex—his favorite.

Meanwhile, Judy Sokol responded to the news of my attention-grabbing homecoming by calling the police to advise them that she had information concerning the case. Judy informed detectives that she knew that I had been living with Hose. She claimed to know this because she had spoken with Justin, and he told her. She offered no reason why she never informed the authorities when they questioned her years earlier, yet she admitted that I had come into her house during the time I was missing and that she had found Hose and me in her bedroom. That was the last time she saw Hose or me, Judy said, since she was interviewed by a CYS caseworker back in 1996 and inexplicably failed to come forward with what she knew.

I believe that Judy had contact with Hose on at least one occasion after that. Regardless, Judy confirmed that she cut and dyed my hair back in 1996. She was presented with a warrant for her arrest shortly thereafter. Judy was not very bright, but I was grateful that she had come forward, regardless of her motives.

As the charges were filed against Hose and Judy Sokol, an international media interest in my story brewed. All of the sudden, my father's phone began ringing off the hook. Calls came flooding in from *Good Morning America, Dateline NBC, Oprah, CNN, Fox News, MSNBC, CBS, ABC, NBC, Geraldo Rivera, Maury Povich, Montell Williams, People* magazine, *Seventeen* magazine, *Jane* magazine, *The National Enquirer,* The Discovery Channel, Court TV, Nancy Grace, Gretta Van Susteren, *CBS 48 Hours,* The Associated Press, German television, Japanese television, and English television, to name just a few. And these media outlets were not just calling. Soon, they were showing up at my father's and Jo-Ann's house. If they didn't come in person, they were sending flowers and gift baskets. It was a hoopla that was briefly part of the celebration that my family and I enjoyed for being reunited. But it was also a hoopla that cast light on Jo-Ann as a loose cannon and my father as an indifferent dad.

My father served me up for some local news-media interviews, but the onslaught was quickly overwhelming, and my father decided to call for help with the situation. Ultimately, I obtained legal counsel to advise me, Lawrence Fisher, and I felt more certain, less alone.

A photo of Tanya at age 17 taken in the room where she was held captive.

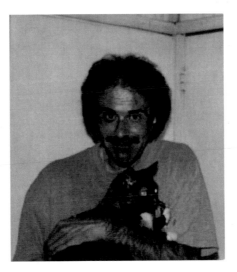

A photo of the pedophile.

A photo of the cats that befriended Tanya:
Max (far left in back), Penny (middle in back)
and Abby (in front toward the right).

A photo of the thrift shop where
Tanya briefly worked before her rescue.

Tanya's side of the room.

Tanya's side of the room (wide view).

Where Justin slept.

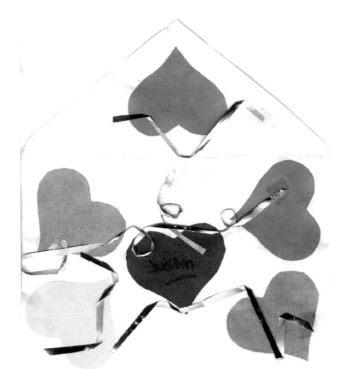

A card that Tanya made for Justin.

Dear Scooter ·
    Just would like to say
Happy Valentines Day. Now I
know Valentines Day is for lovers
and couples etc. But I think its
also for friends too. (I know
you have no friends) so instead
I'll say were chums or pals.
Besides I just like to make and ·
give gifts anyway.
        your chum or pal ·
            Edith ·

Happy
Valentine's
Day!

A card given to Tanya by the pedophile.

Katy
You are
purr-fect
I love you!

Tom

BETRAYED
A LAWYER'S PERSPECTIVE

So it was that Tanya lost ten years of her life. That's all she knew at first. Later she learned that certain citizens of McKeesport participated in an unwitting conspiracy of neglect and incompetence that doomed her to those ten lost years. How could McKeesport authorities not have helped her when they had so many opportunities? Why didn't any staff or faculty do anything when rumors surfaced at Cornell? Where were the McKeesport police? Her parents obviously failed her. Yet where were social services? The system failed her, and nobody cared—nobody except a deranged pedophile focused only on his own needs.

Surely, school security officers entrusted with the responsibility of safeguarding a community's children receive appropriate training. Wrong. St. Moritz did not even advise Hose about his responsibility to report suspected abuse, such as the attempted rape of Tanya by her Uncle Greg. St. Moritz security company, the subcontractor hired by the school district to provide security at Cornell, did not instruct Hose about what to do if a student visited or called him at home. Neither did St. Moritz, nor Cornell faculty and staff, offer Hose any direction whatsoever about what to do when Tanya complained to him that her basic needs were not being met at home, that her stepmother was abusing her, and that her mother was involved in outrageous conduct.

During the time when Hose worked for St. Moritz, and while he was a security guard at Cornell, he never engaged in any training sessions, nor were his abilities ever tested in any way. In short, St. Moritz placed the importance of keeping their business contract with Cornell above the safety of the students. St. Moritz claims the school should have provided guidance to Hose. Someone should have. If so, maybe Tanya's story would have been different.

In reality, Cornell Intermediate School at-large failed Tanya as much as anyone else as is mostly evident from the previously mentioned derelictions by Substitute Principal Andrea Abrams, Administrative Assistant Dan Pacella, and Guidance Counselor Debbie Burnett. Beyond that which has already been disclosed by this book, although they made an announcement to students in connection with the disappearance and abduction of other students such as Anna Marie Callahan and Kimberlie Krimm, no announcement was made regarding Tanya's disappearance. It's likely that her behavioral problems were a headache to school administrators. Her disappearance was probably a relief to Abrams, Pacella, and Burnett.

Furthermore, Cornell had no policy regarding sexual abuse prevention, intervention, or reporting, although state law was already in effect since the 1980s that required teachers and staff to identify and report possible sexual abuse of students. Staff and faculty at Cornell received no guidance, nor any training, about recognizing and responding to such inappropriate behavior. This reckless disregard for the welfare of students was especially glaring because the Chief of McKeesport police in 1996, Tom Carter, also sat on the McKeesport School Board of Directors. Had the school board complied with state law and directed the staff and faculty at Cornell with proper training, requiring them to report incidents such as the one that Hose supposedly admitted to Elias, or the widespread knowledge of the inappropriate relationship between Hose and Tanya on school grounds, there would have been a written report that might have assisted in identifying Hose as a person of interest in connection with her disappearance.

And though the faculty and staff at Cornell will not admit it, the impropriety between Hose and Tanya was clear by the time of her disappearance in February 1996. For instance, her study hall teacher, Donna Kane, actually dated Hose for a period of time. Whenever Ms. Kane knew that Hose was on his way to her room, she would freshen up her make-up. Tanya, likewise, would freshen her make-up. Noticing this, and likely rather jealous, Ms. Kane punished Tanya for putting on make-up in class. Instead, she should have been reporting her suspicious relationship with Hose to others in authority.

Beyond the indifference of Faculty and Staff at Cornell, the McKeesport police demonstrated the most extreme lack of excellence in relationship to Tanya's plight culminating in the unwitting conspiracy by which those in authority discarded her.

Tanya's abused and neglected childhood that preceded her final disappearance with Hose in February 1996 was exacerbated by the incompetent involvement of the McKeesport police that foreshadowed Tanya's ordeal with Hose. For instance, prior to her captivity, Tanya was the subject of two missing persons reports filed with the McKeesport police and within the ambit of Elias' responsibilities, on December 3 and 5, 1995, respectively. The December 3rd report pertained to another sexual assault complaint that was filed with the McKeesport police regarding the incident with Kevin Churchfield that named Tanya as a victim. Regarding this report, no supplemental reports were produced until June 2000. Juvenile Lieutenant E. Michael Elias was all the same responsible for acting on the December 3rd 1995 report implicating Churchfield, and he claims that report was never shown to him.

Churchfield actually provided Elias with further reason to suspect Hose in connection with Tanya's final disappearance in 1996. Police knew that she babysat for Kevin Churchfield's kids. And they knew that Churchfield made inappropriate advances toward her and wrote her notes that contained improper content. So, he was an obvious person of interest to question in connection with her disappearance. In response to questioning by the McKeesport police, Churchfield claims that he told authorities back in 1996 to check out Hose. He claims that Tanya told him about Hose and that he was "...a guard at the school, and she had a big crush on him. . . . She used to brag about that security guard. She'd say she had the biggest crush on him." Elias did nothing in the wake of this critical information.

Elias was oblivious to the fact that Tanya had been the victim of a sexual assault by Kevin Churchfield in December of 1995, and he remained unaware of the Churchfiled report. He claims that this sexual assault report generated by the McKeesport Police Department in December of 1995 would have been available to him if he "...had known it was there" and "...if they had sent it to me." Carter also stated that Elias should have been aware of such a report.

Furthermore, because she often ran away to the home of her paternal grandparents, Elias overlooked evidence from that source as well.

Recall also that Elias was aware of her discipline problems at school. By his admission, "It seemed like every time I went up to the school, she was in the office awaiting disciplinary measures." These interactions were followed by a bungled and botched opportunity for the McKeesport police to have prevented Tanya's captivity back in January 1996.

It was the morning of January 5, 1996, at 3:00 a.m., when Tanya ran out of Jo-Ann McGuire's house to call for help after Jo-Ann threw an ashtray at her. Jo-Ann and Tanya's father had decided to keep her up all night at the dining room table scolding her for bad behavior. Tanya finally insisted that she be allowed to go to sleep. When they refused, she placed her head on the table and said, "Fine, I'll go to sleep right here." That's when Jo-Ann threw the ashtray. It hit the table and broke a glass next to Tanya's head. Shards of glass flew into her hair, and Tanya was cut and bleeding.

She ran from the house. Neither Jo-Ann nor her father even tried to stop Tanya from leaving. She found a pay phone and called Hose. As she was talking to him, a McKeesport police officer drove by and stopped to inquire why such a young girl was out on the street at such a late hour. When she told the officer what happened, he simply returned Tanya to her father and Jo-Ann as though nothing had happened.

This January 1996 ashtray incident was then anonymously reported to Children and Youth Services, a state agency responsible for investigating allegations of child abuse, which began an investigation as to whether Tanya was a "dependent child" for whom state intervention was necessary. Under state law, if she was a "dependent child," a dependency petition was the mechanism by which Tanya could be protected. Essentially, such a petition is filed in state court where a judge reviews the allegations and determines the nature of official intervention necessary to protect the child. Often, these petitions result in removing a child from an abusive environment. Counseling is also and often provided to "dependent" children and their families.

The CYS caseworker assigned to investigate the ashtray incident contacted Tanya's guidance counselor at Cornell, Debbie

Burnett. It just so happened at the time of this call that Elias
was present in Burnett's office on a disciplinary matter related
to another student. Burnett handed the phone over to him, and
Elias proceeded, in front of Burnett, to inform the caseworker
that Tanya was known for "wild accusations," such as the one that
Hose had pointed out to him in the past. He stated his intent to
file juvenile criminal charges against Tanya, which he never filed,
and informed the caseworker he would look into the matter and
get back to her. Then he went to Jo-Ann's home to supposedly
investigate the incident. He spoke with Jo-Ann and Tanya's
father, but Tanya was not initially present for that conversation.
As she arrived home from school that day and found him in the
house, Elias did not even ask Tanya what happened. Instead, he
scolded her and said that he was going to make sure that she
was placed in a state detention facility for bad kids. Afterward,
Elias called the CYS caseworker and instructed the organization
to cease any involvement in the matter.

This incident, as reported to CYS, is documented in a Risk
Management Intake Worksheet generated by CYS about the
potential abuse of Tanya.

1-5-96   12:20 p.m.

***

Lt. Elias stated that he was at the school today
to charge Tanya with disorderly conduct. "*She is
a constant disruption at school.*" *Per Lt. Elias Tanya
has a history of making wild accusations. The C has
made accusations that a school guard tried to "molest"
her in the past.*

Per Lt. Elias, the C wants to move back with the
M so she can do what ever [sic] she wants. The C

knows if she goes back to M, M won't force her to go to school. Per Lt. Elias, I was given to F by the courts because of M's drug history.

The McKeesport Police received numerous complaints from M saying that Tanya is abused [and] tortured by her F, all of which are not true.

Lt Elias stated that he will go to the C's home and look at the C and call CYS back this afternoon.

(Lt. Elias feels C made up the story of being hit with the glass.)

***

1-1-96 [sic]   5PM

TC from Police Officer Elias. . . .There was an argument at the home early this AM. F smashed an ashtray on a table ("to make a point") about C's poor behavior at school.

***

Per officer Elias, NO CYS intervention is needed at this time.

Elias freely admits this conversation with the CYS caseworker in which he stated that Tanya "...was a constant disruption" and had a "history of making wild accusations." Similarly, Elias stated that "I obviously told CYS at that time that I didn't think it was necessary for them to come remove the child from the home." In addition, Elias stated that, based upon his interaction with Tanya,

"There was no need for CYS to rush up to the house or come down to the police station."

Thus, without even speaking to Tanya to obtain her version of what happened, or undertaking a proper investigation into the "ashtray incident," Elias cast a shadow on her veracity in the eyes of the CYS caseworker. Based upon his preconceived notions of Tanya, as well as his prior conversation with Hose regarding her, Elias told the CYS caseworker that she was untrustworthy in that she had made "wild accusations in the past." Similarly, Elias told the caseworker that he felt that Tanya lied about what happened. More importantly, Elias used his position as Lieutenant of the McKeesport Police Juvenile Department to halt any CYS intervention on Tanya's behalf. This happened in spite of the fact that he knew that she was prone to running away, getting into fights, and refusing to heed parental instruction. In this regard, under Pennsylvania law as it existed in 1995, a "dependent child" was defined as:

Dependent child." A child who:

(1) is without proper parental care or control, subsistence, education as required by law, or other care or control necessary for his physical, mental, or emotional health, or morals;

(2) while subject to compulsory school attendance is habitually and without justification truant from school;

(3) has committed a specific act or acts of habitual disobedience of the reasonable and lawful commands of his parent, guardian or other custodian and who is ungovernable and found to be in need of care, treatment or supervision.

Based on Elias' characterization of her, Tanya fit squarely into the statutory definition of a "dependent child." In the course of his conversation with the CYS caseworker, he basically gives textbook reasons why she should have been adjudicated "dependent," yet tells CYS not to get involved based upon the notion that she was not to be trusted. Adding indifference to this injury, when asked whether he ever considered getting CYS involved in Tanya's case prior to her disappearance, he said: "No. At that time, I wasn't aware of dependency petitions. I had to find that out for myself." However, he admits that if he had known about dependency petitions he "more than likely" would have filed one on Tanya's behalf given her circumstances. On top of this, then-Chief of the McKeesport Police, Tom Carter, also stated his opinion that the police and CYS should have worked together in order to, "...get this child into court and find out what's going on here."

It makes little sense that Elias would tell CYS not to become involved when he was unaware of any other procedural mechanism, such as a dependency petition, to protect Tanya's best interests. Rather than simply deferring and allowing CYS to handle the matter, he arrogantly took control of the situation by steering CYS away from any involvement. In so doing, he affirmatively placed her under the bumbling care of the McKeesport Juvenile Division which was completely and totally untrained to deal with such situations. His lack of training and supervision, coupled with his ignorance of the basic procedures associated with protecting the interests of juveniles, only added to the bubbling cauldron of ineptitude surrounding the handling of her case from December 1995 continuing through the investigation of her final disappearance in February of 1996 and onward.

Not unexpectedly, when Tanya disappeared in February 1996 for the last time until her rescue years later, according to what Elias told Hose, Elias seemed relieved that he no longer had to solve the unsolvable problem that he faced with Tanya.

Four days after her final disappearance into captivity with Hose, in February 1996, when a missing persons report was filed with the McKeesport police, Elias fared no better than ever. Tanya's father waited approximately four days to report this disappearance for several reasons. First, he mistakenly believed that the law required a waiting period for reporting a missing person. The law he misunderstood does not apply to juveniles. And when he had reported her missing in the past, Tanya had mostly always returned in two or three days from when she ran away. The officer who originally took down the report did not collect a photo of her because her father's belongings were all boxed up in the wake of his move to McKeesport to live with Jo-Ann. So, he did not have a photo at hand when he filed the initial report. The matter was then assigned to Elias.

Although Elias interviewed her father, the lieutenant's attitude reflected the sort of outright indifference one would expect from a political crony. Elias did not bother to follow up and ask her father for a photo, nor did he collect a photo from the school to place in the file.

Had Elias merely posted a simple stake-out of the area where Judy Sokol and Hose resided, he would have likely discovered Tanya during that first month in February 1996 when she went back and forth between both houses, before Sokol refused to let her visit anymore. And in the days following this disappearance Elias made virtually no effort at the school to investigate.

After Tanya's final disappearance, Elias claims to have interviewed parents, but not students at Cornell, asserting that Tanya had no friends at her new school. No parents recall being interviewed. Had he bothered to ask the school to make an announcement to students regarding her disappearance, however, he would have discovered many who knew Tanya. Monica Krimm, Christine Obradivich, Brandy Donkin, Jeff Loader, Ashley Faust, and Carrie Coulter all were aware of her crush on

Hose and saw that they followed each other around constantly. Indeed, she had confessed to Carrie Coulter that Hose was her so-called "boyfriend." Even Hose's co-worker and fellow security guard at Cornell, Ed Rager, saw her around him "Quite a bit," but Elias never interviewed him either. Elias also did not interview the faculty and staff at Cornell, who all knew about the illicit goings on between Tanya and Hose.

As if all of this is not sufficient condemnation of the McKeesport police regarding Tanya, shortly before she fell captive to Hose in 1996, her paternal grandmother, Beverly Kach, found and delivered to Elias her diary and a scrap of paper that pointed to Hose and Judy Sokol. The scrap of paper merely contained Judy Sokol's name and telephone number. The diary contained a passage that referred to a person named "Tom." The passage referred to a lewd act performed by "Tom," as well as Tanya's reaction to it. Beverly repeatedly called the police to report this information after Tanya's disappearance. Her phone calls were not returned. When she was able to see Elias in person and inquire into the investigation, he told her that she had no standing as a grandparent to be involved in the case. Even the Federal Bureau of Investigation is reported to have looked into her diary, and yet there were no breaks in the case. Mysteriously, the diary is now lacking any pages with reference to a man named "Tom." Jo-Ann also saw this diary and confirms that it contained this reference to "Tom" prior to the time it was turned over to authorities.

About two years later, after Elias was demoted from the case, his successor took possession of the diary. Hose was questioned in connection with the newfound interest in what was then a cold case. The detective who took over, Gene Riazzi, also failed to issue a warrant for telephone records or stake out the Hose house, but he obtained a photo of Tanya. Following the deaths of two other Cornell students, Anna Marie Callahan and Kimberly

Krimm, Allegheny County homicide detectives took possession of the diary.

In the fall/winter of 1996 came the astonishing tip that Elias received from an unidentified informant indicating that Tanya was held up in the Hose residence, and the subsequent McKeesport police presence at the Hose residence in response. Though Hose deflected the investigation, and the police failed to look for her inside the house, the incident obviously made Hose nervous. A few days after this time when McKeesport police came to his house inquiring about Tanya, Hose told her that he inquired about the incident when he spoke with Elias at one of Elias's visits to Cornell on unrelated matters. Elias spoke to Hose about this concern as if Elias had no information why the McKeesport police came looking for Tanya at his house. In Hose's version of this encounter, Elias shrugged his shoulders, turned up the palms of his hands, with his face reflecting ignorance. Hose retold this encounter as if Elias had convinced him not to worry about it by saying, "Tanya's case has been cold forever now. No one cares anymore." Had Elias simply executed a search warrant in response to the tip, Tanya would have been saved early on. Worse yet, had the officer who went to the Hose residence taken Hose up on his offer to search the entire house, Tanya would have certainly been saved.

From 1996 onward, instead of focusing the investigation of Tanya's 1996 disappearance where it belonged, the McKeesport police abdicated their responsibilities to other authorities who decided to concentrate on bizarre accounts of what inconceivably happened to her. For example, in response to her registration in the national database for missing and exploited children, there was a report from West Fort Worth, Texas, that a girl with a nametag reading "Tanya" was working in a check-out line in a grocery store and that she also resembled the photo of her that had been featured on a television show about missing and exploited children. McKeesport police dispatched the police in Lincoln Borough, Texas, to Albertson's, Kroger's and Wynn Dixie's with negative results. Of course, she wasn't there – she was in Hose's bedroom all that time.

Far away in Leon County Florida, they chased a lead from a convicted criminal serving a lengthy prison sentence who claimed to have picked up a hitchhiker in 1998. He said that the hitchhiker had blond hair, and her name was Tanya. He told authorities that he murdered her and left her body in the state game lands near Tallahassee.

Police files indicate that they followed a report in April 1999 where Tanya was reputed to have been seen shopping in a Wal-Mart in Lima, Ohio. Thereafter, in June 1999, they exhibited unusual concern with a supposed sighting in Wyandotte, Michigan, where someone matching her description was seen sitting on a picnic table in Bishop Park. This girl was said to have been kicked out by her parents a few years ago and had been living with her boyfriend until he recently kicked her out. And a report from California August of 2002 added two children to the mix. Other alleged sightings of her were of interest to the McKeesport police when the only place they needed to look was under their noses.

In 2006, when Brandy Donkin was interviewed by the police after Tanya was freed from Hose, she confirmed what Elias should have known. Brandy stated that she and Tanya were friends when they attended school together at Cornell, but she was not aware of Tanya's disappearance. When asked how this was possible, she stated that she was only fourteen at the time, and that she thought maybe Tanya had moved away or that she was no longer attending the school. She further said that if she had been asked by the school, she could have informed them of the relationship between Hose and Tanya, and she confirmed that she and Tanya would often skip class together during school. She stated that one time a teacher caught them and turned them in. However, there was another time when they skipped class and were caught only by Hose. This time, he did not turn them in and, in fact, allowed them to continue missing class. Brandy also confirmed that Tanya told her that she and Hose had kissed before and that they were planning on being together.

Brandy also described how Tanya had a tough school life. She confirmed that Tanya was often in fights at school and often skipped class. She stated that Tanya had been friends with Monica Krimm, but recalled the fight when Krimm spit in Tanya;s face and tore off the necklace Hose had given to her. Brandy concluded that Hose helped protect and cover for Tanya when she was involved in incidents at school – information Elias could have used to solve the case if only he cared. If only someone had bothered to speak with Tanay's friends, at the very least, her ordeal could have been avoided.

The ineptitude of Elias is not surprising when considering that he initially refused to take the position of Juvenile Lieutenant with the McKeesport Police and repeatedly said, "Don't bother me," when asked several times to serve as Juvenile Lieutenant. In 1995 he eventually "...caved in" and took the position. His boss, Chief Tom Carter, "had no hands-on policy" when it came to the supervision of Elias, even though such supervisory authority was vested in Carter

The need for Elias to assume the role as Juvenile Lieutenant arose because in 1993 the police department lost "seventeen of the oldest and senior ranking members...which pretty much destroyed the command structure of the McKeesport Police Department." Apparently, this mass retirement of McKeesport police officers included the Juvenile Lieutenant who held the position before Elias. Despite the fact that Carter was "begging" the ill-equipped Elias to take the position as Juvenile Lieutenant in the wake of the destroyed command structure of the McKeesport Police

Department, he left Elias alone at the helm once Elias accepted the job.

Elias received no specialized training regarding his obligations under state law, of which he was unaware, directing him to report the alleged inappropriate behavior disclosed to him by Hose regarding Tanya. He also similarly lacked specialized training regarding his statutory obligations under state law, of which he was unaware, to immediately report to the school district that Tanya was lost, missing, abducted or runaway. Instead, he reported this to Tanya's school two years after the fact. Among the cascade of flaws that encompass Elias, he never received any specialized training even after he became Juvenile Lieutenant. How is it possible that no one ever requested that he engage in any specialized training? So it comes as no great surprise that he was never tested or observed to evaluate his need for specialized training, and Chief Carter was completely aware of all these shortcomings. Given all of this, it is no wonder that Elias was "overwhelmed" with his position as Juvenile Lieutenant.

Incongruously, official and documented McKeesport policies provided and provide that: "To prepare employees for new assignments, the Department provides specialized training in these areas where a need has developed. . .training may be attended by police officers desiring specialized training. All requests for specialized training should be directed to the Chief of Police." Chief Carter knew of this formal policy, but still never provided Elias with any specialized training.

Noteworthy, too, many complaints were lodged about Elias during his tenure as a McKeesport juvenile lieutenant. He was admonished concerning his failure to utilize supplemental reports in numerous investigations. Additionally, he was the subject of an officer conference regarding compensation he sought for attending juvenile hearings where he had no direct testimony and involvement, yet he never involved himself in juvenile hearings regarding Tanya. Elias was also the subject of an officer conference regarding his duty assignment and warned that communication functions must be maintained during his tour of duty. Alarmingly, a citizen complaint was filed against him alleging that Elias refused to take a gun off a man who engaged in a confrontation with the citizen which Elias observed. He was also the subject of a complaint filed with the American Civil Liberties Union regarding his handling of juvenile investigations. Even Chief Carter criticized Elias for what should have been done in Tanya's case. Is it any surprise that he was ultimately demoted from the position of Juvenile Lieutenant, but not in time to do Tanya any good?

Furthermore, Chief Carter, in his own right, received no training for the position he held as Chief of the McKeesport Chief of Police from 1995 through 1998, nor were his qualifications for that position ever evaluated prior to 1995. And Chief Carter was unaware of his statutory obligations under state law to immediately report to the school district that Tanya was lost, missing, abducted or runaway and he never notified the school district in lieu of the failure by Elias to do so until August 1998.

Chris Cicchitto is a former McKeesport cop who blew the whistle on the way things work in McKeesport. After reading Tanya story, he came forward to take on the McKeesport establishment. He was on the force back when she disappeared. While he learned from other sources about her disappearance, he recalls no indication of a missing persons report that should have appeared on the McKeesport Police 24-Hour Report.

Chris also confirms that promotions in the ranks of the McKeesport Police are tied to campaign contributions to successful mayoral candidates. He claims that this is the way Elias and Carter obtained their ranks and promotions, by corruptly bribing then-mayor Joseph J. Bendel. Although Chris was never directly assigned to the investigation of her disappearance when he was a cop, he was present on the detail that was detached to Hose's house in late-1996. As he was not the officer in charge, he had no say in the decision to decline searching the residence.

After she escaped from Hose in March 2006, Chris investigated her disappearance and found all of the clues that were there for Elias back in 1996 – clues that pointed dead on to Hose.

THE IMMEDIATE
AFTERMATH

I guess I shouldn't have been surprised that those who failed me most ten years ago—the McKeesport Police—immediately began to sling mud in news articles following my rescue. After my story broke, the McKeesport Police and the former juvenile lieutenant that initially investigated my disappearance, Elias, smeared my parents in the press as not particularly concerned with my disappearance ten years before, and they slammed me as well.

Matters were made worse by Jo-Ann's comments to the media about the day I disappeared; she claimed that she woke my father that morning to tell him that I, along with my personal possessions, were missing, but my father just rolled over and went back to sleep. It was difficult enough to make a transition from captivity in the light of a media frenzy. It was hard as hell to do so in the face of the poison that was spewing from Elias and the

McKeesport Police. My father suggested that his attorney could help me navigate my new life in the media spotlight.

I first sat down with my soon-to-be attorney, Lawrence Fisher, four days after my release from captivity. Though my father had prior dealings with counsel over the phone and through the mail, no member of my family had ever met with him before that day. By the time Mr. Fisher arrived, some media outlets had given up camping out on the street where my father and Jo-Ann lived and where I was staying. When he went to the kitchen door and knocked, none of us answered. Then, when he persisted and knocked at the front door, Kevin, Jo-Ann's son from a former marriage, was sent to peer through a curtain he pinched back with one hand.

"What do you want?" he asked.

As soon as Mr. Fisher announced himself, Kevin opened the door and led him to a seat at the family dining room table. As I was summoned by my dad to meet a total stranger, the whole thing seemed beside the point. It was a Saturday. In particular, during my captivity, that was the day of the week designated by Hose for sex. What many take for granted as a pleasurable experience had become a twisted and perfunctory act for me. I grew to hate that day, and the first Saturday after I was freed from captivity, I felt the greatest relief of my life that I did not have to have sex with Hose. This meeting with a lawyer was not the focus of my thoughts. It was hard to focus at all.

When he suggested a lawsuit on my behalf, I told him, "I don't care about that," and, "That's only why you are here." I have to admit, I was distracted by my feelings, as they had evolved in just a few short days since I escaped from Hose. I felt outraged as I increasingly realized how much of my life had been lost to him. By contrast, upon rescue from him, I told the police that I did not have any interest in seeing him punished and just wanted to put the whole thing behind me and get on with my life. As days passed, however, I reflected increasingly upon experiences I had missed—like my high school prom and graduation—during my time with Hose. It upset me to know that I could never go back to the simplicity of a sweet sixteen or slumber parties with my girlfriends. It angered me to think that I was twenty-four years old and had never been out on a proper date, and it broke my heart that I had lost my virginity to this man.

Given all the media attention, my immediate intentions—beyond alerting others to the ways of a pedophile—were to make sure that Hose could not profit from this story and that police and school officials were held responsible. Mr. Fisher suggested that a lawsuit could achieve my purposes. In addition to a contract for legal representation, he presented me with an agency contract for him to act as my spokesman. All of a sudden, this meeting with the lawyer evolved to the point that I was presented with contracts that represented the most significant decisions I'd had to make since my rescue. It was overwhelming.

After executing legal documents, the first order of business was to prepare for a bond hearing to meet with Laura Ditka, the assistant Allegheny County DA, who was prosecuting the cases against Hose and Judy Sokol. Ditka is the daughter of legendary Chicago Bears Coach Mike Ditka and is every bit her father's daughter. A big woman and a bruising prosecutor, she made her career placing child molesters behind bars. Ambitious at heart, she intended to be a judge someday soon—and a conviction in the mega-high-profile case against Hose could certainly aid this ambition. Sparks flew immediately upon this first meeting with her.

Originally, bond was set for Hose in an amount that he was unable to pay. He was seeking a modification that would allow him to post a bond to ensure his presence at all legal proceedings against him and would allow for his release from prison while charges against him had yet to be proven. The thought of him at liberty in the community frightened me. At the very least, my

lawyer suggested that we insist on bond conditions for Hose that
provided for his electronic monitoring by authorities and house
arrest. But I was summoned to the prosecutor's office on the day
of the bond hearing solely to go over evidence relevant to the
hearing, and Ditka had no idea I would bring my attorney. Ditka
did not even expect me to attend the actual bond hearing; she
simply wanted to meet alone, without counsel, prior to the bond
hearing to discuss the case generally. As introductions where
exchanged and Ditka realized that I had brought my lawyer with
me, Ditka balked.

First, she politely asked him to leave the room while she met
with me. When he asked why this was necessary, she offered up
a lame justification about the presence of a third party to her
meeting with me might require her to turn over to the defense
her notes from the meeting. My lawyer pointed out that other
third parties, such as the detectives investigating the case, as
well as my father and Jo-Ann were already present in the room,
and that Ditka's notes would likely require disclosure to Hose's
defense regardless, which is why prosecutors usually do not take
any notes at such meetings.

Ditka got angry and declared, "Unless Tanya and I can meet
alone, I'm not going to proceed with the bond hearing. My
problem," she continued, "is that I can't control you, Mr. Fisher."

It was immediately apparent that Laura Ditka was upended
by the possibility that another attorney might bend the limelight
away from her. No such intention existed. The limelight bends by
a force of its own ordaining origin. My lawyer assured her that
he had worked quite well in the past with other assistant district
attorneys in her office and that he would not interfere with this
prosecution in any way. As she balked some more, I began to
think that it was important to have someone looking out for me
and that this prosecutor might have more than just my interest
at heart. After all, Ditka had just threatened not to pursue the

bond hearing as a means of excluding my counsel from this meeting. Though I was still reeling from my ordeal with Hose, I was mentally sharp enough to perceive the friction between Mr. Fisher and Ditka in terms of what was best for me.

"I'm not going to proceed without him here," I said.

Ditka realized that her threat to cancel the bond hearing was empty. She had to do her job.

With that, the bond hearing for Hose proceeded as scheduled. Afterward, the new conditions of his bond confined Hose to house arrest with an ankle bracelet for electronic monitoring during the remainder of the criminal proceedings against him. The hearing caused a swarm of media coverage, but I was secreted in and out of the courthouse by my lawyer, protected from the media as much as possible. After the bond hearing, I met with county detectives and Mr. Fisher to discuss the process by which the criminal cases against Hose and Judy would proceed and my protection would be further ensured. As much as I should have been protected from Hose, I needed just as much protection from many facets of my newly emerging life.

After the bond hearing, Laura Ditka was increasingly difficult, and my difficulties in otherwise adjusting to life post-captivity got worse. First, I was attempting to catch up on all the schooling I had missed while held captive by Hose. Additionally, I had obtained my learner's permit for operating a car and was studying to earn a driver's license. But Jo-Ann would not let me practice with her car, and my father found many excuses to avoid taking me out to practice in his car. I knew I was quickly becoming an inconvenience to him, and some of the old feelings of sadness came back.

At the same time, I was enrolled in a GED program, but transportation was still a problem. I could not access public transportation due to the notoriety surrounding my case. Without a car, I was surviving on the generosity of my family, friends, and meager public assistance from the government. Mr. Fisher was driving me everywhere and even let me practice driving his car. To this day I still remember vividly what a white knuckle ride that was for my lawyer. He was a good sport about it. Still, this was no way to live, but I was grateful to him. I had gone from being a psychological captive to being a financial one. Finally, my mom paid for driving lessons, and I earned my license in short order. In a desperate attempt to garner the resources to purchase a car from a charity auction, I considered granting an interview to German Television. As a courtesy, Mr. Fisher provided notice of this interview to the prosecutor's office. Laura Ditka went berserk.

Even though the interview was not to air in the United States, Ditka called a halt to it. She claimed it would have been a "disaster" and accused me of being "dumb like a fox."

At one point during the criminal proceedings against Hose, Ditka caused a two-month delay by failing to have certain paperwork in order. Much to my anguish, she did not even extend the courtesy of alerting me, nor did she ever contact me in any caring way.

Then, when my financially destitute situation left me with no choice but to file a civil lawsuit against those responsible for my situation, the McKeesport Police, school district, St. Moritz, and others, Laura Ditka went off on another rage. Though she had been given advance notice of the lawsuit and provided with detailed reasons why it was necessary to file it, she nonetheless shouted that she was "not happy." She offered no suggestion for a solution to the financial and emotional hardship I was suffering, while her office refused to investigate the claims raised by my civil lawsuit—claims including official criminal corruption by the McKeesport Police surrounding my disappearance. By contrast, Lawrence Fisher obtain a car for me from a charity auction.

Regardless of Ditka's ambivalence about my adjustment difficulties, she nonetheless pressed on zealously with the prosecutions of Hose and Judy Sokol. Less than two weeks after the bond hearing, a preliminary hearing was scheduled to determine whether authorities had enough evidence to go forward with the charges against Hose and Judy Sokol. I was a nervous mess. The charges were serious, but as Laura Ditka also described them, "smart." Instead of charging Hose with kidnapping, and thereby providing him with an opportunity to drag me through the mud as having been a runaway, he was charged with statutory assault, statutory deviant assault, corrupting the morals of a minor, interfering with my custody, and other related offenses. Under Pennsylvania criminal law, basically all the authorities had to prove to convict Hose on these charges was that he and I engaged in certain sex acts when I was less than sixteen years old and when Hose was eighteen years old or older. All they needed to prove against Judy was that she helped him. I was the only other person besides Hose, and perhaps Judy Sokol, who had first-hand knowledge in this regard, so my testimony at the preliminary hearing was crucial.

The key test of whether these charges would go forward, therefore, was my ability to take the witness stand and testify about such desultory matters. It was a shaky time for me. I met with Lawrence Fisher and the detectives handling my case before the preliminary hearing. The thought of confronting Hose face-to-face in a courtroom terrified me. Everyone involved on my side of the situation tried to make this day as easy on me as they could.

On the morning of the preliminary hearing, Mr. Fisher picked me up at my father's and Jo-Ann's and drove me to a secret location near the courthouse. There we met again with Greg Matthews and Ed Fisher (no relationship to my lawyer), the two Allegheny County detectives who were handling my case. These detectives provided a private police parking lot adjacent to their meeting place for me. From there, my lawyer and I were whisked into the courthouse by a special entrance for police personnel so as to avoid the media crush. Two grief counselors, also called victims' advocates, where present to literally hold my hand in and out of the courtroom, shielding me from the only place where cameras where allowed near me. Even the cameras in the court hallways were court ordered to stay back twenty feet. My entire family sat in the row of chairs behind me for support. My paternal grandparents, aunt, and cousin came in from Alaska to be there for me. Upon being called to the witness chair by Ditka, I felt my right hand tremble as I swore to tell the truth, the whole truth, and nothing but the truth, so help me God.

Initially struggling to keep my voice up, I testified as to the gory details of the crimes Hose committed against me. I confirmed that our first kiss was at Cornell Middle School under the gymnasium stairwell and that afterward, I continued to have a "personal, more intimate" relationship with Hose. The attorney for Hose complained that he could not hear my testimony. So did the attorney for Judy Sokol. And the court actually acknowledged difficulty hearing what I was saying. Finally, I said, frustrated, "I can't help it. I was quiet for ten years."

As I raised my voice, I proceeded with devastatingly blunt testimony that outlined the extent to which Hose's perversions revealed him as a predator and pedophile. All the while, unknown to most in the courtroom, I was ripping off my acrylic nails one by one in a fit of nervous energy and dropping them on the floor of the witness box. In the end, when I stepped down from the witness chair and sat by Geraldine Massey, my victim advocate/ grief counselor in the courtroom, Geraldine asked, "Where are your nails?"

I pointed to the witness box. "They are up there."

As the preliminary hearing wound down, a sheriff deputy observed Hose cock his head ninety degrees to glare at me, and I could feel his cold eyes burn through me.

I looked back at him without hesitation and screamed, "Don't look at me."

At that point, a sheriff deputy positioned himself between us, so as to block me from his sight. The hearing ended shortly thereafter, when Magistrate Judge Donald Preusuitti had no choice but to order Hose and Judy Sokol to stand trial on all charges.

When it was over, I was quickly rushed from the courthouse, again protected from the media, and returned to my father's home, where I watched in disbelief as television reporters all over the world went on and on about the event. I felt a similar fear and helplessness as I had on September 11, 2001. Mentally exhausted, I knew I had much more to endure.

NEW BEGINNING, NEW PROBLEMS

During my captivity, I did not once receive any sort of medical attention whatsoever. Upon my release, I required urgent medical care, among other daunting challenges. Two of my teeth were badly decayed, and I needed root canal surgery, as well as two crowns. I had eight other cavities that required fillings. The root canal procedure went poorly because the dentist provided by public assistance was a hack. I developed an infection and was briefly hospitalized. Afterward, I changed dentists, and my new one had to redo the root canal altogether because the first dentist had done a bad job.

An MRI and CT-Scan confirmed that I suffered from problems with my spine, born of poor nutrition and a lack of physical activity while I was maturing into adulthood in Hose's bedroom. And all of this was on top of the scars from untreated psoriasis while I was captive, as well as diminished vision resulting from untreated pink eye. Chest pains, migraines, anxiety, fits of shaking, and a host of other physiological problems plagued me. Yes, I was free, but not from the memories or miseries.

I immediately began intensive treatment and therapy. I was diagnosed with adjustment disorder, post-traumatic stress disorder, and obsessive-compulsive disorder. A good part of the time, I suffered crying spells, and some of the time, I felt downhearted and sad. There were times during my first year free from captivity that I did not feel useful or needed. Because I did not have a job and really could not have worked at that time even if a job had been offered to me, I had no resources other than public financial assistance. As a result, the clinic where I received therapy was not a well-respected or well-staffed facility. I went through three therapists, as turnover at the clinic was high. Finally, Janice Pope, a private psychologist, agreed to provide therapy free of charge. Although the steady therapy from Janice was helpful for a time, she turned out to be a glory-seeker and abandoned me in the long run. It seemed as if my situation brought out the worst in some people, especially people who were supposed to be professional.

For instance, renowned talk show host Dr. Keith Ablow called me constantly and repeatedly asked me to appear on his national show, but he would not offer me any therapy unless I agreed to be part of his psychiatric circus act. Any of these problems would have been hard enough on any twenty-five year old woman, but the circumstances surrounding me heightened my difficulties.

Most stressful were the legal proceedings that loomed ahead. A resolution of the criminal charges against Hose was far in the future. Meanwhile, a federal civil lawsuit had been filed by Mr. Fisher and was pending on my behalf. It alleged that my captivity should have been prevented by the McKeesport Police, the McKeesport School District, and others. But it, too, was awaiting a determination on its merits and whether I could bring suit for my damages under such circumstances. All of the information I was called upon to reveal for the pursuit of these civil and criminal legal proceedings upset me. I felt a deep invasion into my privacy, one that challenged my determination to tell a cautionary tale that might save others from a similar plight. I ultimately summoned the might to reveal my ordeal as I have, but only after intensive prayer and introspection. Beyond this, even other issues plagued me.

In the first year after my release from Hose, I was mentally hypersensitive to the world, and my world was not the same as it was for others. On the street, random strangers called me out with rank resentment. On one occasion, two big men in dark suits appeared out of a black Cadillac Escalade and began photographing my car in front of JJ's. When Joe Sparico approached these men and attempted to determine their purpose, they sped away like goons. Obscene and suggestive letters addressed to me arrived from unknown people across the county. Blogs were dedicated to debating my story. Sometimes I would receive unsolicited gestures of support from people I had never met before in my life; other times, however, people would go out of their way in attempts to harm me.

An auto repair shop, for instance, tried to rip me off when the ball joint in my car needed to be replaced. They charged me to replace it, but I later learned that they had, in fact, charged me for nothing and allowed the dangerous condition to remain. When I confronted the owner of the shop, he refused to accept responsibility and said only, "You are a very infamous young lady."

Even Beulah Park United Methodist Church, the church that I attended in McKeesport during my last ten months of captivity, turned its back on me. I was told by the pastor in no uncertain terms that I was no longer welcome there. Though the church would not officially prevent me from attending, I was told it would be best if I stayed away, as the publicity that surrounded me was unwelcome. As much as this hurt my feelings, I was able to join a Methodist church in Elizabeth, where I was living with my father and Jo-Ann. Even so, life was not without many wary moments for me.

I was the unhappy recipient of affection from a McKeesport man I knew through the Sparicos. All of a sudden, this man began attending my new church in Elizabeth. He was twice my age. He always went out of his way to sit next to me at church or approach me after church to talk. He even moved from McKeesport to a place directly across the street from my church in Elizabeth. This balding, gray-haired man was becoming obsessive, and he often approached me when I was having conversations with others and interrupted with random nonsense.

I knew that I was obviously overly sensitive to attention from men, and I tried to be nice. Then at Christmas 2006, I heard that he was bragging to people about a gift he bought for me. I was shocked when he gave me an expensive diamond tennis bracelet. It was too much. I feared that I was being stalked.

Finally, I mustered the courage to cross the street from my church, go up on his porch, and knock on his door.

When he answered, I told him, "I can't accept this."

After a short exchange of words in which he tried to convince me to keep the bracelet, I threw it into his home, onto the floor, and stormed away.

By contrast to my troubles, by the end of 2006, I had obtained the education I missed while in captivity with Hose, and I was enrolled in college, studying business. My new life was emerging. My first Christmas free in ten years was overwhelmingly joyful for me, despite all of my struggles. The holiday of hope found me in the sanctuary of my church, family, and friends.

My faith and spirituality strengthened amid widening possibilities for my future. Christmas 2006 was wonderful. I joined my church choir, and I sang with vestal voice every Sunday. My grandpap, Jerry Kach Sr., attended a couple of my choir practices, even though my father refused. I was thrilled my grandpap came to see my loving participation in the Christmas cantata, where choirs from all over gathered to sing together. Then there was Expressions, a woman's group I joined through my church. As part of that, I was thrilled to have a so-called "secret sister," to whom I gave a special and anonymous gift. These may sound like small pleasures, but they meant everything to me.

My church activities and Christmas celebrations were many. Despite the fact that I repeatedly asked my father to share the holiday with me to no avail, I helped decorate my church for Christmas, and when the holiday was over, I helped take down these decorations. I also served food at the church holiday lunch. I attended and frequently still attend Bible study on a weekly basis. I used every last bit of my limited funds to buy gifts for everyone—my mother, father, Jo-Ann, Craig, Kevin, Joe, Jan, Joelle, Brianna (Joelle's young daughter), even my cat (I rescued a cat from a shelter)—everybody. And I spent time making Christmas cards for all of those around me. I mailed them out with a photo of me in my choir robe and felt blessed and joyous for whatever lay ahead.

During this time, I remained uplifted by my relationship with the Sparicos. I spent more and more time at JJ's, helping out with everything from stocking shelves to running the cash register. After my mother helped me get a better car, I gave the charity auction car to Joelle. With the Sparicos, I was able to share my feelings and struggles in a loving environment, and they will always be family to me. They stayed by my side from the very outset of my rescue from Hose, and it was they who convinced me to get a new cat when I started to miss the feral ones I had left behind with Hose.

I tried to be positive and focus on my new life that justified a new pet. When I got one, I named it "JJ Jobri." "JJ" for the initials of Jan and Joe as they appeared in the name of their store, JJ's

Deli Mart, and "Jobri" for the combined names of Joelle and her daughter, Brianna. In the end, however, Joelle was always around only when the cameras came around. She kept insisting that I schedule an appearance on Oprah when she knew that I did not want to do anything of the sort. She even began to express crazy suspicions about my appreciation for all her father did to help rescue me from Hose. Jan did not seem to talk to me unless it was about the subject of my lawsuit. Nevertheless, I realize that no person is entirely good or bad, and the Sparicos will always have a place in my heart.

I can't say which celebration or gift was most important to me that holiday season. I very much benefited from being in college. And every day was like Christmas from that fateful day of March 21, 2006.

On my first day of college, I was a little nervous, and I did not know my way around all too well. Still, I was excited to be there. I never imagined that such a day would arrive, and I was proud of myself. In college, I began making friends and meeting all sorts of interesting people. A few people on campus recognized me from images seen on television, but largely, my fears never materialized about being called out as I had on the streets of McKeesport. I began to experience a better world, and my emotional progress began to show. Yet for each moment of progress, there were as many setbacks.

RIGHT BACK
WHERE I STARTED

Family issues, among others, added to my problems after I was technically free. In some respects, I found myself right back where I was before I ran away at age fourteen. My mother and father despised each other and often attempted to tear each other down in front of me. My mother, however, was counseled by many about dealing with my difficulties. She arose as a source of financial and emotional support for me in the time after I escaped Hose, though we had our difficulties. In any event, as I developed a deeper relationship with her, my father became resentful. That, coupled with the financial pressure that came from having another person living with him, caused him to act in ways that were not supportive.

He attempted to control my comings and goings, which I outright rejected. He also criticized me for undertaking so much therapy and refused to speak with my therapist or attend any therapy sessions. Although I knew I was becoming defensive toward him, I couldn't help it. *This can't be happening to me again,* I thought. *Not after all I went through. I won't ever be controlled by anyone again.*

Jo-Ann pretty much ignored me, giving me the silent treatment, while my father even began to question my story, mostly because Jo-Ann became jealous of me. My father claimed that he never doubted that I was a victim, but he was having a hard time understanding what happened to me all those years.

"I want everyone involved to do right by my daughter," he said.

Yet he was upset by the way my relationship with Jo-Ann spoiled in the year that followed my return to him. To this day, I maintain a fondness for my father, all the same. Forgiveness is forever when it comes to family. Even though I now understand that he is a negative force in my life that should be limited at all costs, I care about him. Regardless, living with Jo-Ann and him was a flashback from the past, and I would no longer tolerate it. Ironically, about ten months after I was free from Hose and I'd returned to my father, I finally achieved what I had wanted so much, so many years ago. On January 14, 2007, I moved in with my mom.

This decision was a pivotal moment in my efforts to leave my ordeal behind, though it would not be so apparent at first. Jo-Ann had been interfering with my ability to heal. She was offended because I was spending time with my mother at all.

She displayed her displeasure most of the time by ignoring me, but when she spoke to me at all, it was with vile intent. She would express skepticism about why I never escaped from Hose all those years, and she used all of her influence to set my father against me. Indeed, I moved out of their home in large part to avoid this hostility.

It was obvious that Jo-Ann began to envy the promising future that was beginning to appear on my horizon as my therapy seemed to be elevating my mood and motivation. When I was moving out, she erupted in a jealous rage, and I experienced yet another hasty departure. We argued and exchanged harsh words in front of Joelle Sparico. Joelle said Jo-Ann was literally "foaming at the mouth," and that about describes it.

Then, after I moved out, Jo-Ann was downright juvenile. She trashed the room where I had been staying, and if it were not for my father's intervention, would have thrown out the items that I had left behind and intended to retrieve later.

When I returned to pick up the remainder of my belongings, I found that Jo-Ann had scrawled, with nail polish, the word *not* under the label on a bottle of Vera Wang perfume that I left behind. The perfume was called Princess. I realized then that she was the same person she had been from the day I had met her. She had not grown, had not moved on. And I had.

Her spite prevented her from calling me when my father was subsequently hospitalized and operated upon to remove his gall bladder. When I learned from my paternal grandmother, Beverly, that he was in the hospital, I rushed to be with him, but Jo-Ann would not let me near his side.

Still, I had hope that moving in with my mother and step-father, Craig, would provide a more supportive environment in which I could face the challenges still awaiting me, such as the upcoming criminal trials for Hose and Judy Sokol.

Nearly a year had passed since I had escaped from him, and as the criminal trial approached, in February 2007, I was not as anxious as I had been for the preliminary hearing. I was ready to do whatever was necessary to see that Hose was punished, and I continued to feel more balanced. Whereas previously I was insistent that he receive a prison sentence of at least ten years, the same amount of my life I feel he stole from me, my views evolved as the trial approached.

Initially, Laura Ditka was suggesting a plea bargain whereby he would serve between seven and a half and fifteen years. I realized that it would be better for him to plead guilty than to go through the ordeal and uncertainty of a trial. Also, through a plea bargain, I would not have to miss as much of my classes at college. Although I was doing my best at dealing with the legal proceedings that became a part of my ordeal after my escape from Hose, it was not easy.

I vividly recall the time I went to Laura Ditka's office to discuss a possible plea bargain for Hose. I brought Joelle along with me for moral support. She sat through the meeting in total silence. Ditka tried to obtain my consent to a plea bargain with him, but I felt strongly that he should spend as much time in jail as he'd kept me from real life: ten years. Besides, under the law, he faced possibly more than forty years in prison if he pushed for a trial and was ultimately convicted. Ditka offered up reason after reason why a trial should be avoided at all costs.

As a funny aside, Mr. Fisher was unable to attend because of another commitment out of town, but he sent a representative from his office and called me after he thought the meeting would have concluded. The meeting, however, was delayed, and when he called, my cell phone went off with the theme song from the television program *Law & Order*, the ring-tone I had specially designated for him. When Ditka realized that he had such a personal and flattering ring-tone, she was unable to conceal her envy. In a subsequent conversation with me, she asked, "By the way, what's my ring-tone?"

"Um, I don't have one for you," I said.

Ditka nearly pouted. "I want a ring-tone too."

That day, however, she had one focus. She claimed that members of a jury might have the same difficulty that my father and Jo-Ann were expressing in understanding why I never left when I seemingly had countless opportunities to. She cited my pending federal civil lawsuit as something that could be used by Hose to dampen sympathy toward me and paint me as a gold digger. Despite copious evidence, a confession from co-defendant Judy Sokol, and incriminating statements from Justin Hose, Ditka hammered me with concerns about jury nullification— the phenomenon where jurors chose to implement an emotional result and find a criminal defendant not guilty despite evidence and law to the contrary. She even suggested that I might not be believed.

She would not offer a single reason in favor of a trial. The subject of punishment for Judy Sokol never arose, and I was not too concerned about her. Ditka instructed me to give it some thought and get back to her. After Joelle and I left this meeting, Joelle said, "That woman scares me."

After excruciating delays, the scheduled trial date for Hose arrived on February 12, 2007. I woke at 5 a.m. to ready myself for this day. A plea bargain was expected. Ditka had convinced me to accept an even less-harsh sentence than she had suggested at our last meeting. Now she told me that Hose would plead guilty to all charges and receive a prison sentence of between five-to-fifteen years in the state penitentiary. In other words, Hose would be eligible for release from prison on parole in as early as five years. Though I still felt in my heart that he should have served a minimum sentence of ten years, I relented to a plea bargain to put the criminal proceedings behind me.

I had prepared some remarks and intended to address the judge prior to sentencing. I arrived, as I had previously, at a secret parking location in downtown Pittsburgh. Although my lawyer had in the past driven me from McKeesport to the preliminary hearing, for trial I was secure enough that I drove myself into downtown Pittsburgh and met up with him at the secret parking lot. There, he led Joelle and me into the courthouse and Laura Ditka's office. Upon arrival, Ditka told us, "There has been a development." Then she dropped the bomb.

Hose had stabbed himself six or seven times and was in the hospital. In fact, the subject of his killing himself was the topic of my conversation with Mr. Fisher and Joelle during the walk over to the courthouse a few moments earlier. Although this news shocked the community, I was not surprised. As long as I had known him, Hose was a dark and suicidal man. All that surprised me was the method he used, that he had not attempted suicide sooner, and that he was so ineffective in his effort. It was later reported that the stab wounds were rather superficial. Though it was not at all Christian of me, I was almost angry that he hadn't succeeded. The coward had managed to delay his ultimate fate.

Even as a troubled teen, I had soon realized that Hose was mentally disturbed, although not in a way that kept him from realizing that holding me as his puppet was wrong. Almost everything he did in reference to me—including his suicide stunt—indicated that he knew his actions were wrong. The suicide attempt also appeared to be a last-ditch effort to avoid paying for his crimes.

In my opinion, he could not afford to mount a psychiatric defense to the numerous criminal charges he faced, so by faking his suicide, he was able to secure a state psychiatric evaluation. He hoped to fool everyone into believing that he had some psychiatric condition that, under state law, absolved him from his crimes if he was incapable of understanding the difference between wrong and right. The media described him as suffering from depression. Who in their right mind would not be depressed at the thought of five-to-fifteen years in jail?

Hose's feeble suicide attempt really sealed his fate. His bond was completely revoked because he purposefully rendered himself unable to comply with the subpoena for his presence at his trial, so his bond was revoked, and he began a long stretch of his own personal captivity. Initially, he was sent to a secure psychiatric facility for evaluation because of his suicide attempt. Once again, by some quirk of fate, I was free while my captor was now a captive of the Commonwealth of Pennsylvania. It was, nonetheless, a let down. I had anguished over the plea deal and was eager for some closure to get the criminal proceedings behind me. Delay was not my friend, but a new trial date was another three months away.

After Ditka delivered this news, she asked us to remain in her office while she tended to a court hearing scheduling the next events in the criminal proceedings.

The courtroom was packed. When Hose's suicide attempt was announced, the crowd released a collective gasp. Media fatigue seemed to overcome the judge, and a gag order was promptly issued.

Ditka was intent on keeping my lawyer from further contact with the media, and she berated him in front of Joelle, as well as many others. Even though he was never served with a copy of this gag order, given an opportunity to oppose the gag order, or directed by the judge that the gag order applied to him, Ditka seemed to lose her head over it. She insisted that the order had been entered because of Mr. Fisher's comments to the media were supposedly harming the case against Hose. In actuality, it was the attorney representing Hose, James Ecker, who requested the gag order in open court. Ditka chose to ignore this reality and railed on against any further comment to the media by my lawyer. Joelle turned to me and said, "Better him than me."

Why Ditka carried on as she did is a mystery to me. Could it have been only about her judicial ambitions and desire for the limelight? It made no sense that she would seek to interfere with efforts to cast me in the media as a true victim. Former and current members of the McKeesport Police had already smeared me in the media. Regardless of the way in which my federal civil lawsuit provided Hose with an argument that there was a financial motive to my testimony in the criminal matter against him, Mr. Fisher explained to me that this argument would have surely been advanced regardless and had nothing to do with the gag order issued in the criminal case against Hose. After all, if Hose was convicted of crimes against me, a conviction would surely help in my lawsuit regardless of my lawyer's comments to the media.

Whatever motivated Ditka to act in ways that, at times, really ticked me off, when she wasn't making me angry, I liked her and felt relaxed around her. Sometimes I even found the sparks between Ditka and Mr. Fisher to be musing. "It's funny how you two bicker like children," I told him. "The other day, Laura called you a blabbermouth."

Laura Ditka was able to regain professionalism at important times after I filed my civil lawsuit. I had repeatedly requested all of the information the prosecutor's office possessed regarding the criminal case against Hose. I wanted to use it against him and in a civil lawsuit against those responsible for my captivity. Laura Ditka resisted providing this information but ultimately did so, gustily declaring, "This information is all covered by the gag order."

At the pivotal moment when the plea and sentencing for Hose finally arrived, Laura Ditka was by my side and a real pillar of strength and support as I read a victim impact statement. In the end, in spite of all the criticisms and shortcomings I could dwell on, Laura Ditka is a good person who helped more than she hurt, and I have love in my heart for her.

FAMILY ISSUES, SOCIAL PRESSURES, OTHER KIDS AND CASES

As the time after my captivity and rescue accumulated, I attempted to cope with all the conflicts in my life with good humor and by pouring myself into college and tending to my many medical needs. This was hard, and family issues, as well as social pressures and some surprising developments, made it an even more difficult time.

After the botched pseudo-suicide attempt by Hose, my relationship with my father began to deteriorate badly. He stopped taking my phone calls and would not return my messages.

Instead, he used his stepson, Kevin, to call me to inquire about the federal civil lawsuit.

Then Beverly, my paternal grandmother, began to call, asking about the federal civil lawsuit and to take up for Jo-Ann.

"You don't love your family," she told me. "You're selfish."

For crying out loud, I thought. *This is the woman who had me declared dead after I disappeared so she could cash in on a life insurance policy she had on me, and I don't love my family?*

"I'm tired of it," I told her. "Don't call me anymore."

Although I still retain my relationship with my grandmother to this day, I was downright frustrated enough with her at that moment that I just lashed out.

At this time in my life, I'm sure I was on the brink of a nervous breakdown and wanted to check myself into a mental hospital, *just to take a vacation*, I rationalized. I was so upset that I just wanted to sit and cry, something I was not allowed to do for many years with Hose. With the exception of September 11, 2001, Hose would throw a fit if I shed tears over anything. So I would cry late at night after he was passed out.

I remembered being a child and the way my mother would hold and comfort me when I cried. *If only my parents could relate to me like that*, I thought. *That's all I want.* At this juncture in my life, I began to realize that my present-day existence was much more stressful than I had ever imagined it would be in comparison to how much stress I experienced living with Hose all of those years. I recognized that I was depressed and found it tragically ironic that he was being treated for depression in a state mental hospital as he awaited his new trial date.

I steadied myself with deep breaths and long conversations with Mr. Fisher, Joelle, and my therapist. Just around this time, the Social Security Administration declared me "disabled," and I was able to realize some relief in the form of greater government resources for my needs. *Maybe, just maybe,* I thought, *now I could rent an apartment for myself and get away from some of the strife.* It seemed that no matter where I turned, I was confronted by problem after problem rooted in all I had endured up to that point in my life.

When my family was not presenting me with so many adjustment issues, I was often confronted by my notoriety in unfortunate ways. At college, one of my professors began treating me harshly for no apparent reason. I had been making friends and trying to enjoy my life a bit. I even began studying with some of my fellow students and going out to lunch with them after class.

Still, Dr. M. J. Richey seemed to have it out for me. The woman was on a real power trip. She refused to discuss my concerns about the way I was being treated and said, "I know who you are."

I reported this to the dean of students who, in turn, counseled my new friends to steer clear of me because, "She is nothing but drama."

I had to file a report with the college vice-president of Academic Affairs so that I could be treated as a student rather than some girl on the news.

As I dealt with the numerous difficulties in my life, I nevertheless maintained a certain grace based in my spirituality. The first anniversary of my freedom from Hose passed without as much as any mention of it in the media. This pleased me. I attempted with every bit of my being to press on with my education at college undeterred by problems there and elsewhere.

At church, I began additional volunteer activity as a waitress during the Lenten fish fry. I donated my tips to my church collection plate each Sunday and continued to pray for peace in my life. As Palm Sunday 2007 approached, I welcomed my first anniversary with my new church in prayer and worship.

I realize that my story is unusual and disturbing, but I know that I am not alone in triumphing over all that I had to overcome.

Just prior to the pseudo-suicide stunt by Hose, something remarkable occurred that served to highlight the unique nature of my story as a cautionary tale in the sad modern history of child abduction cases. In January 2007, world news broke out of Missouri about the miraculous discovery of Shawn Hornbeck over four years after he was reported missing at the age of eleven. The Hornbeck story followed a similar news cycle as mine.

At first, it was just a miracle, but soon it became questionable why Hornbeck did not escape his captor. Because Shawn Hornbeck was never sequestered from society and appeared to be living willingly with his captor, people could not figure out why he did not flee in the four years after he was abducted. I am convinced that Shawn's abductor probably controlled him in ways similar to the ways that Hose controlled me—with fear and psychological tactics.

There were common contentions of death threats in both cases. Both Shawn and I come from susceptible backgrounds. Shawn did not appear to have known much of his biological father, if at all, and I was damaged when I was separated from my mom after my parents' divorce. And just as it had when news of my story broke, the hungry media descended on Shawn Hornbeck. As the story played out, and as I observed the developments, I had only one thought: *My heart goes out to that boy. I know exactly what he is going through. Few others ever live to tell about it.* In my wildest dreams, I would love to meet Shawn, give him a big hug, and let him know that I understand why he didn't leave his abductor.

Outside of custody disputes between parents, only about ten cases in modern history have occurred in which children abducted for lengthy periods have lived to tell about it. Many similarities can be observed, but one case from Japan seemed most like mine. Fusako Sano is a Japanese girl who was only ten years old when she was kidnapped and held in captivity for more than nine years by a mentally disturbed loner named Sato Nobuyuki. Nobuyuki, like Hose, lived with his mother, who did not know about Fusako Sano for most of her ordeal. Also, the door to the room where Sano was held was not locked, but she was threatened and lost the energy to escape. Sano had no bath or toilet where she was confined and was only allowed to take a bath infrequently. Further similarities stem from the fact that Nobuyuki also engaged in a failed attempt to avoid his crimes by bemoaning his mentally disturbed state of mind. There were also criticisms of the police investigation regarding Sano's disappearance.

In these rare child abduction cases where the children are later found alive, the bonds can be both psychological and physical. For example, the case of Natascha Kampuch was reported throughout the world from Austria in August 2006, just five months after I escaped from Hose. When she was ten years old, Natascha was held captive and confined for more than eight years in a windowless and hidden room. An armed steel door was an impossible barrier to her escape.

Another of these rare instances involved Colleen Stan, also known as "Carol Smith." She was abducted in 1977 and held until 1984 in locked wooden boxes.

As far as we can tell, the first known case that might be characterized as a child sexual abduction goes back to nineteenth-century Germany. There was great gap before the first case reported in modern history came out of California in 1980, regarding Steven Stayner. The Stayner case involved the psychological captivity of a young boy when he was only seven years old. Here, too, Stayner seemed susceptible to his abduction. He was the brother of a convicted serial killer. Likewise, the crimes committed against Stayner were sexual.

Additional rare cases like mine were reported in 2003, concerning a Belgian child, Sabine Dardenne; in 2004, concerning a United States child, Elizabeth Smart; and in 2004, concerning two young Russian girls.

Then, in June of 2007, it happened again. If the Shawn Hornbeck case was unusual in its proximity to mine, news broke out of Connecticut that caused me even more flashbacks to my own ordeal. Police in West Hartford, Connecticut, discovered Danielle Cramer, who had been missing for almost a year. She was found in the home of Adam Gault, who had been hiding her and allegedly carrying on a sexual relationship. As in my case, Danielle was said to have dyed her hair and assumed an alias. Likewise, it was claimed that Danielle was a runaway and kept a diary of her sexual affairs with Gault. The big difference was that the police in West Hartford did their job and investigated Danielle's disappearance, whereas the police in McKeesport did almost nothing to find me.

In 2009, I experienced another flashback when I read about the case of Jaycee Dugard. She had been abducted in California eighteen years earlier, when she was eleven years old. Jaycee was held by a man and his wife, and her captor fathered two children with Jaycee.

In these long-term abduction cases, particularly the cases of Hornbeck, Cramer, and myself, many wonder why these children don't simply escape the situation. In at least these three cases, none of us were physically restrained.

Eminent psychologist Lawson Bernstein explains how someone in that predicament can remain so for such a prolonged period:

Tanya was already a psychologically troubled and abused youth prior to the events in question, and therefore particularly at risk for further abuse and control by any adult bent on subjugating her. She was sexually abused/tortured and de facto abducted by Hose at the age of fourteen. Thereafter, Tanya was continuously subjected to this highly abnormal, abusive environment, in which her limited adolescent capacity for judgment and associated free will was subjugated to the undue influence of her adult captor. She was deprived of anything approximating a normal and/or nurturing home life during the tenure of her time with Hose. The highly abnormal and abusive environment described above was inimical to any type of further emotional, cognitive, or other critical developmental maturation in Tanya from age fourteen onward. Based on the above highly abnormal and continuously abusive state of affairs, Tanya was bereft of her cognitive faculties and associated capacity for normal adult judgment such that she was unable to fully appreciate the nature of Hose's abuse of/control over her and to take steps to actively interdict that control and associated abuse.

What the experts fail to examine is my belief that cases of children being held in psychological captivity are not randomly grouped within the past three decades. Instead, I think that many other children were abused this way between the isolated case from Germany in 1828 and the first to come after it in 1980, when Steven Stayner escaped his captor. Indeed, I believe that these cases are a sign of the times. The difference, in my opinion, is that the world is getting smaller, and we are more vigilant in our modern world, but we are still not careful enough. My case certainly offers proof of that.

I think we have a tendency, as a society, to write off our more troubled kids, but that these are exactly the children that we must offer even more attention and care. I worry that children from ideal backgrounds who perform well in school are less at risk than the rebellious youth we tend to marginalize. Pay attention to all of your children, especially if they are troubled. These are the kids who wind up in horrible nightmares no one can imagine.

Finally, I feel that our attention must focus on what happens after the miracle that occurs when missing children are found. As my story relates, it's not just happily ever after from there. There's so much to deal with, particularly the underlying family issues that made these kids susceptible to their ordeals in the first place. Then there's the stress of legal proceedings and the media. On top of this, a certain sort of arrested development occurs as a result of these situations. Let me tell you, because I've been there. The focus should be more on how to help families cope in the wake of such trauma and less on questioning the actions of children in these circumstances.

HIATUS

The new trial date for Hose and Judy Sokol was May 14, 2007. In the hiatus between Hose's suicide attempt and the new trial date, life marched on in a rhythm that continued to be characterized by progress and problems.

I was truly sick and tired of being recognized. Invariably, when I was out and about, shopping, enjoying a craft fair, or for whatever reason, people would approach me and say, "Aren't you that girl?"

They would tell me that they recognized my eyes, that my eyes are absolutely unforgettable. Others knew me from my long blond, flowing hair.

I faced deep conflict with public recognition. Although I did not wish to deny who I was, I had done that for more than a decade. On the other hand, I just wanted to be left alone. And the weird thing was that I found myself in a flashback to my life around February 1996. If I would just cut and dye my hair, I probably would not be as recognizable. And so, in one way, I wanted the same thing I'd wanted more than ten years ago; only now, I did not want to deny my identity by cutting and dying my hair as I had back then. This twisted reality was even more problematic when I considered that writing a book would likely feature my image on the cover. Moments like this made me feel sad and lonely with my problems.

All the same, I vowed never to be controlled again, not even by my circumstances. Though I blamed myself for making a bad decision in the first place when I ran away to Hose so many years earlier, I was nevertheless determined to hold my head up high. *Yes, I made a mistake, but I got through it, and I'm doing what I have to do. I have goals.* I knew what I needed to do to make my own happiness in life. So, I began volunteering at a senior home during the summer, after college was in recess. Otherwise, I spent my days at JJ's, waiting on customers. I enjoyed the company and conversation, and I needed the support that the Sparicos offered, especially as May 14, 2007 arrived.

On May 14, 2007, in a drenching spring rainstorm, I arrived at the courthouse late for yet another trial date that Hose would evade. I was taken to a secluded room, where I waited in vain for the criminal case to finally proceed. In the wake of his prior suicide stunt on the eve of his last trial date, I still remained hopeful that he would plead guilty this time and spare me the ordeal of a trial. Yet, I was prepared for a trial if necessary.

Laura Ditka greeted me with uncertainty about the trial. Since Hose's recent pseudo-suicide antics and his subsequent commitment to a state psychiatric hospital for evaluation, it was unclear whether his evaluation was concluded. Without an evaluation concluding that he was at least competent to assist in his criminal defense, his trial could not proceed. Furthermore, he awaited a full evaluation that might conclude that he had a psychiatric condition that afforded him some sort of defense to the criminal charges against him.

I told Ditka that regardless of the determination to go forward or not, I wanted to be present in the courtroom to observe whatever happened. She ignored this request, with nasty consequences.

Ditka and the defense attorneys gathered before Judge John A. Zottola, who had been presiding over the Hose and Sokol criminal cases all along. For the first time in all the proceedings against Hose up to that point, his parents, Eleanor and Bud, were present in the galley. His attorney blathered on about his client's suicidal ideation, etcetera. Hose had yet to be deemed competent to stand trial. Ditka saw no point in going forward against just Judy Sokol if Hose was still not competent. In actuality, a plea deal was in place with Judy, regardless of whether Hose accepted a plea deal. The deal for Judy was simple; she would cooperate and testify against Hose, throw herself on the mercy of the Court, and Ditka agreed to take no position on whether the court would impose jail time. This plea deal notwithstanding, Ditka did not want to proceed with resolving the charges against Judy, because it would alert Hose to the deal with Judy for testimony against him. He might figure that any testimony by Judy against him could be viewed as motivated by her deal with Ditka rather than the truth. This might embolden him upon gaining competency to insist on trial in lieu of a plea because Judy's testimony against him would be tarnished by her plea, thereby diminishing the case against him.

All the legal wrangling aside, the judge set a new trial date for Judy and Hose for June 26, 2007 and ordered that a medical report be provided regarding his mental state prior to that date. After hours of waiting in a secluded victims' room, I was informed that Hose was still not competent to stand trial, that a new date had been set for his trial, and that the proceedings for the day had concluded.

I was angry, and not surprisingly, most of my anger was directed at Ditka. I was incensed that she was not up to speed on developments in the case to know and advise me beforehand that Hose's evaluation was incomplete and that trial would not proceed. More important, Ditka had completely disregarded my request to be present in the courtroom as the matter was discussed and decided. After the proceedings had been continued and the parties dispersed, I was informed that I could leave and go home.

Instead, I stormed into Ditka's office and wagged my finger in her face. "Why wasn't I brought into the courtroom as I requested?"

Ditka was obviously taken aback but calmly stated, "I was trying to spare you the media."

"That's bullshit, Laura," I retorted. "The media is outside your office right now. They just chased me down the fucking hall all the way to your mother fucking office!" Before Ditka could get another word in edgewise, I added, "Next time, I want to be in the courtroom, no matter what. That is my right. Are we clear?"

Ditka exhaled deeply.

TURBULENCE GIVES WAY TO HOPE

The days that followed were full of stress, starting with my mother. Out of nowhere, she began questioning me about my federal civil lawsuit. She had become acquainted with a local gad fly attorney, the fat and obnoxious Rose Turzak, who was filling my mother's head with delusional notions about how badly my federal civil lawsuit was being handled. Lacking an iota of professionalism, Turzak undertook a transparent attempt to chase glory and convince me to fire Mr. Fisher so that she could take over my federal civil lawsuit. All sorts of threats ensued. First, Turzak threatened to intervene in my federal lawsuit. Then, she threatened to have me deemed incompetent and have my mother appointed as guardian so that she could control any money received from my federal suit.

This caused me unimaginable stress. I held my ground against my mother, who, at one point, told me I would have to move out if I did not allow Turzak to take over my lawsuit. The Sparicos reassured me that I could live with them and they would watch over me, if necessary. Fortunately, Turzak was not even admitted to practice in the federal court where my suit was filed.

Turzak ultimately found an attorney who was, at the time, admitted in the federal court and who was willing to take a look at second guessing the legal work already performed in my lawsuit. She was sorely disappointed to hear his opinion that my lawyer was "doing a great job." Still, this was no great compliment but a further rebuke to Turzak, as the attorney that Turzak selected to review my suit went on to file a totally baseless lawsuit on behalf of my mother against the McKeesport Police. Indeed, my mother hired Arnold Y. Steinberg to file a federal civil lawsuit on her behalf against the McKeesport Police that was ultimately dismissed. Mr. Steinberg was subsequently disbarred for stealing from his clients before the unsuccessful resolution of the case he thoughtlessly filed on behalf of my mother and against the McKeesport Police.

Attorney Steinberg's decision to file a federal lawsuit against the McKeesport Police on behalf of my mother traveled a path of thoughtlessness that had a negative impact on me. Too much time had passed since my rescue from Hose. Immediately after my rescue, it became readily apparent that he should have been discovered by the McKeesport Police as the perpetrator all along. By the time a lawsuit was being contemplated by my mom, over two years later, it was too late under the law to bring a claim.

The misguided theory on which Steinberg sought to pursue a suit on behalf of my mom was one where she was somehow harmed by the harm visited upon me by Hose and the failure by the McKeesport Police to prevent this harm. This was nonsense, as she was every bit as responsible for inflicting harm on me during some of the time when Hose harmed me. I was incensed by her undertaking to file her federal civil lawsuit and wanted her stopped.

It was clear that all my mom cared about was money. I felt that she was acting with delusional disregard for the way she abused me as a child. And although I had come to peace with the harm my mom had caused me—and had forgiven her—she, however, offered no reconciliation as to her past behavior toward me.

It was decided that various documents from the 1995 custody proceedings when she was ordered to have no contact with me would be sent to attorney Steinberg. He had to realize the true nature of the person with whom he was dealing.

By what happened next, I can only surmise that attorney Steinberg was wavering about whether to represent my mother in a separate suit. He must have revealed his knowledge of the abuse I suffered from her as a kid. She and my step-father, Craig, went crazy. As I lay in bed at two in the morning, I awoke to hear Craig ranting and raving about my "mother-fucking lawyer" and my "mother-fucking father." The screaming woke me up, and as I went to use the bathroom, Craig came storming at me, shouting, "I want you out. Now!"

"It's two in the morning," I replied.

"I don't care. I want you out!"

I was sick of this, and in exasperation, I said, "Just shut up."

Craig was incensed. He was now screaming even louder. His veins were bulging in his neck. "You don't realize how afraid of me you should be!"

"I'm not afraid of you," I said. "I'm not afraid of anyone."

Craig stepped toward me and raised a clenched fist.

"You should be," he told me.

That was enough for me. I went to the phone and dialed 911. Before the operator could take any information, however, my mother, who had observed everything, grabbed the phone and hung it up. An operator called back. Craig answered the phone. I could hear the operator ask if everything was all right. Craig said, "Yes," but in the background, I shouted loudly, "No, please send a car!"

When the police arrived, my mom immediately alerted them to the fact that I was "The girl missing from McKeesport."

I wondered what on earth that had to do with anything. One of the officers recognized me. We all went inside to talk, and Craig acted as if it was all a misunderstanding. The situation was calm for the moment, and the police left me in the presence of this danger, as had happened to me so many times before.

The next day, my mother and Craig continued out of control. Craig was off his rocker about the supposed lies that my lawyer was spreading about my mom. Now, instead of threatening me, he told me that if Mr. Fisher did not apologize by the end of the weekend, he would meet up with him in an alley somewhere and beat the shit out of him. Again, Craig insisted, "I want you out."

My worst fears had been realized. I called Joelle, but Joelle would not let me come and stay with her, offering some phony excuse about being on public financial assistance and having to follow certain rules about how many people could be in her government-subsidized apartment. That never stopped her boyfriends from staying there. Nevertheless, I packed some things and called my father. He would not let me stay with him either, but later he would lie and claim that I never asked. Instead, he agreed to take my cat for a couple of days.

I dropped JJ off and headed over to Joe Sparico.

"I'm homeless," I said with tears pouring down my face. "Tell me, where do I live?"

Joe was prepared to put me up in a hotel room because of the turmoil my situation was causing in his family. His wife, Jan, was very upset about having to deal with my problems all the time and did not seem to understand why all of my problems were placed at her doorstep. Why, for example, didn't Mr. Fisher take me in for a couple of nights? That was, in fact, a consideration, but we feared the headline, "Kach Shacks Up with Lawyer."

Exasperated, Jan called my mom and prevailed upon her to take me back for a couple of days while I searched for housing.

The next day, I drove into Pittsburgh to the Center for Victims of Violence and Crime. I met with Mr. Fisher, as well as Geraldine Massey, the victims' advocate who had been providing me with counseling and guidance about the criminal justice system from the outset after I escaped. I was provided with myriad phone numbers and appointments for evaluating affordable housing options. Within an hour, I was meeting with Ciera and Kate, two student volunteers with National Student Partnerships, at Duquesne University in Pittsburgh, who cut through the red tape and filled out necessary forms as they searched for me to find a place to live. Still, any relief from living with my mom would likely take days, and Joelle was not accepting my calls. Hurt and alone, I feared that I would have to stay in a shelter for homeless women.

Later that day, as I continued the process of finding a place to live, my mom and Craig calmed down and said I could live with them again. The tides began to turn in a more peaceful direction for me in the days that followed. I began therapy with my mom. In weekly sessions, I realized that she had blocked from her mind all of the times she'd abused me. The therapist and I decided that the best way for a breakthrough was to actually show her all of the documents from court proceedings that demonstrated the terrible things she had had done to me.

My mom is not a woman prone to crying, but when she reviewed these documents, she broke into tears. She could not believe what she had done. In black and white, the incontrovertible proof let her apologize profusely to me and to finally accept responsibility for her actions. We were finally on the path to a positive relationship.

I came to realize that she cared for me in her own way. I also recognized that my mother was as prone to "Make a mountain out of a molehill." We agreed to cease our ceaseless debate about past abuses that had been inflicted upon me. And I realized that I could not demand that my mom forego a lawsuit against the McKeesport Police if that is what she wanted. She was an autonomous human being with a right to bring a legal action in her own name if she so chose.

Thereafter, my paternal grandparents traveled to visit from Alaska, and my paternal grandmother, Beverly Kach, was being more supportive and comforting than she had in the past. In addition, the time that I was spending with my grandparents served as an escape from my mother and Craig and, often, the world at-large.

Then, a former judge learned of the difficulties I was experiencing and donated some money to help me find a place to live. And just when I needed some good news the most, I learned that Hose had been deemed competent by the state mental institution where he had been treated and returned to jail. At long last, a day of reckoning for Hose seemed a certainty. When Joelle heard this news, she finally called me, and now she was interested in traveling with me to his trial, probably because she would be seen on the television coverage of the event. But I didn't care. As was so frequently the case in my ever-changing life, turbulence gave way to hope.

SILENCING THE SKEPTICS, NAYSAYERS, AND CYNICS

For Hose, justice was served on a day in June as sweltering as the many I spent in his bedroom. As I walked through the halls of the courthouse and into the courtroom, cameras flashed wildly, and I was flanked, as always, by my lawyer, Joelle Sparioco, and Geraldine Massey from the Center for Victims of Violence and Crime. The comfort I felt as I held Geraldine's hand was as special as any for which I could hope.

It was as if life was preordained for Geraldine Massey to work as a victims' advocate in the criminal justice system. Back in 1993, Geraldine lost two of her sons to gun violence. It was the Center for Victims of Violence and Crime that helped her make sense of the Pennsylvania criminal justice system after the murders of her sons, Omar and Gerald. She is the poster child for victims' rights. In the course of her odyssey through the criminal justice system for the murders of her sons, Geraldine sat through the selection of eight juries. She watched five mistrials, two first-degree murder convictions, and one acquittal. As if that were not enough, her first husband, Omar's father, was convicted of second-degree murder in 1976 and was sentenced to life in prison. She is a remarkable survivor who turned her tragedies into a powerful and positive force for transforming the lives of others.

Remarkably, Geraldine was not bitter. As she puts it, "Counseling is the answer. No one should be held back by grief." If anyone could serve to show me the path past my grief, it surely was Geraldine Massey.

As she accompanied Mr. Fisher, Joelle, and me, everyone took their seats in the front row of the public seating in Judge John A. Zottola's courtroom. This time, I arrived at the courthouse and went directly to the courtroom instead of Laura Ditka's office. I did this on purpose in light of the way Ditka had decided to shield me from the proceedings in the past. This time, there was no way I was going to miss one minute of these proceedings because of her. In fact, just a few days prior, she'd called and said that Hose would only agree to plead guilty and avoid a trial if I agreed upon sentence for the guilty plea of five-to-twelve years in prison, as opposed to the previously agreed upon term of five-to-fifteen years.

"No way," I told her. If that was now the supposed deal, then I was no longer on board and would protest in favor of a trial. Ditka got the message and put the deal back on track at five-to-fifteen years in prison, which I had agreed to accept. When I asked her how she had managed to convince him to accept three extra years to his sentence, Ditka said, "I just waved my magic wand."

Seated behind me in the courtroom was my paternal grandmother, Beverly, my Grandpap, Jerry Sr., as well as my father and Jo-Ann. For the first time in the proceedings, my mom and Craig did not attend.

For a brief moment, there was some concern that Judy Sokol was going to renege on her plea bargain and insist on a trial, but that matter was postponed, and Hose was brought to the courtroom with his feet and hands shackled. He was dressed in a dark business suit. The shoulders of his suit jacket were caked in dandruff. As he passed the throngs of cameras in the hallway, he made an odd gesture, flicking the tip of his nose with his index finger, as if he were communicating some secret code to someone who might be watching the news coverage. He had made this gesture at almost every prior criminal proceeding he'd attended. This was just another strange gesture from a strange man.

While sheriff deputies brought him into the courtroom, and as he shuffled past me, Mr. Fisher placed himself between us as a barrier in case Hose lost his mind or decided to do something stupid. He just scuffled pathetically past us and up in front Judge Zottola. There, he listened as Laura Ditka read the terms of the plea bargain by which he admitted his guilt as a child molester and predator. Hose was about to plead guilty to all of the charges against him.

Before he admitted guilt and was sentenced, I was permitted to give a victim's impact statement. Approaching the bench from my seat in the courtroom galley, I was just four feet from him, and I faced him as Ditka stood between us. From a prepared statement, I addressed Hose directly:

I just want to know why you did what you did to me for ten years. Why? You took away my innocence, my childhood. Made me think my family didn't want me or love me, that no one cared or loved me but you. Made me think that you were the only one in the world for me.

For ten years you dominated me, controlled me, what I ate, drank, what I wore, how I looked, how I acted. It's so sad to say, but I was a puppet, nothing but a puppet. I really don't know if I can ever forgive you for what you've done to me. But mark my words, I will let people know in due time exactly what you've done to me. I want people to know the kind of monster you really are.

But there's some things I want to let you know—I am standing here a completely changed person. I am not that dominated puppet anymore. I am a very independent woman who has a lot of self confidence. Remember how you always used to say to me 'oh, you're just a pretty face, you're stupid, you're not going to get anywhere in life, you're nothing without me?

Well let me tell you I'm not so stupid. I got my GED in just seven months. Just finished my first semester in college with very good grades. I plan on making a success out of my life. I plan on going places, and I'm going there without you. But the main thing I want to do is help protect children and women from men like you.

I know that God granted me the strength to get through what I endured from you for a reason. Now you get to know what it's like to need that same kind of strength, but you don't get to ask for it. Because I get to say to you what you've said to me so many times quote "shut up I'm talking" end quote and don't ever forget God hates ugly.

I sobbed, and my voice quivered at times while I read my statement. Laura Ditka wrapped her arm around me, gave me a tissue, and comforted me.

Hose muttered repeatedly, "I'm sorry, I'm sorry."

I silenced him by shrieking, "Don't you apologize to me!"

Judge Zottola then turned to Hose and asked him if he had anything to say before he sentenced him.

"I want Tanya to know how sorry I am. God only knows how truly sorry I am," he told the judge. "Over the last fifteen months, the thing I play over and over in my mind is that Ms. Kach told me, 'Thank you. If it wasn't for you, I'd be dead or in the street.'"

This drew a strong rebuke from the judge, who said he had considered rejecting the plea deal but recognized that a trial would be painful for me. The judge retorted, "I think you give yourself too much credit." Then he sentenced Hose to serve a period of incarceration for no less than five years and no more than fifteen years in a state correctional facility. He would be placed on a registry of sex offenders and would never be allowed to work at a school or with children ever again. A sheriff deputy then led him out of the courtroom and back to jail. His fancy suit would be replaced by an orange prison jumpsuit for at least the next five years.

Judy Sokol's appearance in court that day was next and much less consequential. She pleaded no contest, or *nolo contendere,* to several counts against her, including interfering with the custody of a minor. Sentencing was deferred until September as the judge considered leniency. Judy remained free on bond and likely would have faced no more than a term of probation until she later failed to express remorse about her role in my abduction and abuse. I bolted from the courtroom hand in hand with Geraldine, Joelle fast behind us. I had no interest in speaking with the hoards of media awaiting me. I had said everything I wanted to say in the courtroom and exactly to whom I wanted to say it. The rest, I trusted to my lawyer. He prepared and read a statement I had approved: "Tanya Kach is relieved to have these criminal proceedings behind her and to have Thomas Hose behind bars. She looks forward to seeing justice fully served in a federal courthouse." He added, "An eye for an eye, and justice is blind for the better."

The skeptics, naysayers, and cynics had been silenced. After the guilty plea, I noticed a much more positive reaction to me on the streets. I received a lot of good feelings from strangers. My fellow church parishioners greeted me on the following Sunday with open arms and a warm outpouring of support and congratulations. Everyone was proud of the way I had shown the strength to confront Hose in court and move on with my life. I was proud of me too.

PEAKS AND VALLEYS
OF RECOVERY

At the conclusion of the criminal proceedings against Hose, as usual, there were immediately unexpected and unfortunate developments. These were becoming the norm; however, I was able to handle matters increasingly well. Outside of the courtroom, my father announced that he would be holding a press conference later in the day at his home. Some of the media flew into a frenzy. He pulled me aside and said, "I'm going to enjoy my moment in the spotlight. It's my turn too." While I wanted my whole family to join me in a celebration luncheon, my father could not attend because he had to hurry home for his hastily arranged press conference. I was absolutely confounded by my father's actions and comments.

Although I was not present, I saw my father's remarks all over the television that night and in the newspapers the next morning. Aside from disclosing publicly where I was attending college, thereby violating my privacy and revealing something that I had guarded with great care up to that moment, he upset me more than he could imagine.

Most upsetting, he boasted about my progress since my release from Hose as if he'd had anything to do with it. He did not provide me with one iota of financial support after I escaped from Hose. Following my rescue, when I lived with him and Jo-Ann, I had to pay them for that privilege. I still remember how, when I asked for help learning to drive, my father mustered only two feeble attempts to teach me, and Jo-Ann didn't want me driving her car. It incensed me that he would claim such credit for my progress when, after I earned my driver's license, and only after my mother paid for my driving lessons, I had asked my father for financial help to buy a car, and he flatly turned me down. He also refused to help me when the car my mom bought me broke down.

I was angriest of all that my father lied about denying me a place to live when I was about to be homeless because of problems with my mom and Craig. How dare he claim that I never asked to come back and live with him?

If anything, he hampered my progress by ignoring me, questioning my ordeal with Hose, and discouraging me from receiving counseling. As far as I'm concerned, all he wanted to achieve in that press conference was for me to become a sex-slave celebrity so that he could benefit from it.

Thus, it was outright insulting to me when he claimed during his celebratory press conference to be serving as a support system for my future. Nothing was further from the truth. When I had tried to share my college papers with him, he said that he was not interested. When I pleaded with him to come see me sing in the church choir, he said he was not interested. When I invited him to visit me at the Elizabeth Methodist Church fish fry and have a meal with me, he said he was not interested. He rarely ever even called me on the telephone and repeatedly ignored my calls to him. Our relationship after my escape had gotten worse.

On Tuesdays, my father's regularly scheduled day off from work, I repeatedly stopped by to visit with him and just spend some time. He was distant and cold. The visits became shorter and shorter, because he simply had nothing to say. Then, on one of my last visits during the summer of 2007, I shared my feelings with my father about something that was very personal to me.

"You know," I said, "I'm not sure if I ever want children of my own."

"I don't want none either," he replied.

I was shocked and angry. "You have one," I fired back.

He smirked. "No I don't."

There was absolutely no reason for my father to make such a snarky remark. He was just being a jerk.

This enraged me even more. "You asshole," I shouted, "you've got a fucking daughter. Me."

He didn't reply and continued to sneer, so I did what I always had done. I left.

Much of my summer therapy sessions in 2007 were dedicated to my father's rejection of me. I had to accept him for who he was while allowing myself to be whatever I wanted to be. Still, I could not help myself from wondering where I would be if Hose had never abducted me. I wondered if I would have a better relationship with my father if not for all I had gone through with Hose. Those and other questions plagued me.

Hose was right when he called me a "wild child." He gave me what he called "discipline." Would I have gained that discipline on my own? I wanted to marry someday, and I wanted to have a normal, loving relationship with a man. Was that now more or less likely in light of what I had been through?

For all of my questions about life, I am sure of certain things: I am not ashamed. I do not feel sorry for Hose after all the nasty things he said to me and after all the things he made me do. I know that I made a mistake by going with him in the first place, but that's the past. I look to the future with some core understandings about myself.

I recently made this list about who I am.

1. My favorite color is pink.

2. I love cats.

3. I am a very emotional person.

4. I take things very seriously (I don't have a tough skin).

5. I am a dedicated person—dedicated in friendship, dedicated in work.

6. I am a survivor in life in general.

7. I've got a lot of love to give; I am a very loving person.

8. I have a "lead foot."

9. I like junk food.

10. I am very feminine.

11. I smoke too much.

12. I like rap music.

13. I am addicted to Pepsi.

14. My dream car is a Cadillac.

15. I'm trying to get through life without medication.

16. I love my church and the bell choir.

17. I didn't panic when recently facing adversity.

18. I love to talk on the phone—I sure like to talk.

19. My ring tone for my lawyer is the *Law and Order* theme music.

20. I'm feisty.

21. I like go for long drives with the music blasting. It relaxes me.

22. Music by Eminem brings me up when I am down.

23. I'm inquisitive.

24. I'm responsible.

25. I love nature.

So I guess I'm just a normal girl, a girl who counts her blessings. I am so appreciative for every little blessing in my life. I take nothing for granted, not the sunshine, not the birds singing outside, not the simple ability to get up and walk out the door freely. For most people, such appreciation for the little things in life would be remarkable; for me, I think it only underscores how much I have been forced to struggle with *all* things in life.

TRUE COLORS

My struggles continued on even after Hose went off to jail, but I was able to handle my problems ever better.

Although the criminal proceedings against Hose had been resolved with finality back in June 2007, because Judy Sokol handled the charges differently than he did, she had a further criminal proceeding to come. Judy's no contest, or *nolo contendere*, plea to certain criminal charges against me meant that she denied guilt but acknowledged that the evidence against her was strong enough to convict, and this complicated matters. Judy was seeking leniency from the court and hoped to avoid jail time. Thus, even though she entered her *nolo contendere* plea at the same time Hose entered his guilty plea, Judy was not sentenced that day. Instead, she requested a pre-sentence investigation into her claim that special circumstances in her life and regarding her crimes merited leniency in her sentencing. This caused the media attention to linger on the case.

A few months later, after the pre-sentence investigation and when Judy was ready to be sentenced, her lawyer's mother was ill, and a postponement occurred. More media attention followed.

Finally, on November 28, 2007, Judy Sokol went before Judge Zottola, but she did not find the leniency she was seeking. The judge was immediately abraded by Judy's *nolo contendere* plea; he observed that she had previously and totally admitted to the police that she concealed my identity back in February 1996, and she also admitted to the police that she was aware of the inappropriate relationship that Hose had with me.

The incongruity between Judy's statements to the police and her *nolo contendere* plea did not sit well with the judge.

"You've got some explaining to do," he told her.

Judy was incoherent.

The judge asked her if she wished to withdraw her plea.

Judy began muttering meaninglessly, and the judge briefly recessed the hearing. After a brief recess, he repeated his request that Judy explain herself.

Once again, Judy was incoherent.

After offering her another chance to withdraw her plea, the judge declined leniency and sentenced Judy to serve six to twenty-three months in a county jail with four years of probation thereafter.

Media coverage of the event was widely circulated on the local news venues. I was grateful to see that the criminal justice system had yet again vindicated the crimes against me. Nevertheless, I was preoccupied by the fact that my grandpap, Jerry Kach Sr., had been diagnosed with terminal cancer two days earlier.

I was devastated. My grandpap and I had just picked up where we'd left off ten years before after I got away from Hose. Our relationship was one of the most important and supportive in my life. Unlike my father, my grandpap never questioned me about what I experienced with my captor. He would listen to me as I described my troubles with my father and my worries of life in general. He would soothe me with kind words of understanding and hope.

He had been married to my grandmother, Beverly, for more than fifty years. My grandpap used to be a butcher in a butcher shop owned by his parents and where Beverly used to shop for meat and other items. One day, Beverly had purchased some cottage cheese from the butcher shop, and as she was leaving, she dropped the cottage cheese, which burst out of its container all over the floor. My grandpap came to her aid, and it was love at first sight.

I had always hoped someone would love me like that one day. I had cherished our relationship. His illness landed on me heavily and hard. I couldn't imagine life without my grandpap. As I worried about and prayed for him, I still had my federal civil lawsuit looming unresolved.

Key to this litigation, counsel for the defendants were eager to depose me, something that I was well aware would occur. In scheduling my deposition in early 2008, however, a wrinkle arose that caused me great stress, and the reverberations from that occasion were significant.

It turned out that the defendants in my lawsuit were demanding that my deposition be recorded on videotape. I was terrified. I had endured vast exposure to the media, and the thought of enduring a video tape of my deposition for all to view in the media was a shocking and unwelcomed event that I could not stand.

Mr. Fisher filed a motion to protect me from a videotaped deposition. The lawyers for all sides engaged in extensive discussions about a resolution to the deposition at issue that would satisfy the interests of all involved. It's not quite clear why the defendants pressed so hard for this videotape. In fact, in and of itself, the matter of my deposition and whether it would be videotaped attained a swarm of media attention as local reporters trolled the federal court docket.

Mr. Fisher's argument against the videotaping of my deposition relied heavily on the opinion of my then therapist, Janice Pope, that such an event would be traumatizing and could trigger terrible psychological consequences for me. In response, the defendants submitted an expert report by an esteemed psychologist that totally refuted Janice's opinions. Janice was outraged at the way in which her opinions were utterly discredited, and she responded by lashing out at Mr. Fisher for reasons that were absolutely thoughtless to my way of thinking. Thus, amid the drama that surrounded videotaping my deposition, Janice injected even more drama and insisted that I fire the one person I truly trusted. He and I were undeterred. We moved forward, together.

Finally, the defendants agreed that the videotape of my deposition would be strictly confidential—subject to a confidentiality agreement signed by all parties—and the controversy evaporated with anticlimactic media reports that the judge presiding over the federal civil lawsuit dismissed my request for protection from a videotaped deposition. Here, the media got it completely wrong. I had won. My videotaped deposition would never be seen by anyone unless I decided otherwise. In the process, however, the relationship between Janice Pope and me suffered, whereas the relationship between Mr. Fisher and me had made it through another bump in a seemingly endless stretch of road. He would be called on to do so over and over again.

As the litigation progressed, the various defendants decided that they wanted to take my mom's deposition. They had no idea what she would say about the facts surrounding my captivity with Hose. They wanted a chance to place my mom under oath and swear to provide testimony that would be recorded by a stenographer and preserved for the litigation. The defendants were particularly interested in knowing what my mom had to say about the call I made to Hose from Craig's house so many years before, as well as the telephone conversation my mother had with Hose while he held me captive. The defendants also seemed intent on using my mom to harass Mr. Fisher. They had seemingly spoken informally with my mom prior to the deposition and became aware of her resentment of my lawyer because he would not file a lawsuit for her and had helped me attempt to block the lawsuit that Arnold Stienberg ultimately filed for her. Here's part of an exchange between one of the defense lawyers, Mr. Fisher and my mom:

Q: Did Tanya tell you that Mr. Fisher told her to exaggerate things?

A: Mr. Fisher told all of us, when he came to our house, "I'm going to exaggerate the truth. You have to exaggerate the truth," which means lie.

This statement by my mom caused incredible upheaval in the legal proceedings, and it only got worse when my lawyer tried to clear things up with my mom.

Q: I would like to ask you about that. You used the word "exaggerate." You claim that I told you to exaggerate in this case. Is that a specific word that you recollect or is—?

A: Yes.

Q: That is the word that you recollect me using, the word "exaggerate"?

A: Exaggerate the truth.

Q: When did I say that?

A: Craig says it every day now. He thought it was a good catch phrase, so I can't forget it ever.

Q: So is it Craig that remembers me—

A: Yes. I do, too, but Craig says it every day to remind me.

Q: That I told you to exaggerate the truth?

A: I'm sorry. I'm sorry. He likes to mock you, so he says it almost every day, "Exaggerate the truth."

The defense lawyers pounced on this exchange and demanded the deposition of Craig, as well as Mr. Fisher and another deposition of me. They were convinced that my lawyer was engaged in the equivalent of suborning perjury, or coaching witnesses to lie under oath.

After my mom's deposition and pending Craig's deposition, the allegations against my attorney caused great stress in my relationship with my mother, but Craig surprised everyone and was able to put the matter to rest. After his deposition, in which he disavowed any effort by Mr. Fisher to encourage any person to exaggerate as it pertained to my federal civil lawsuit, the federal judge presiding over the case refused to allow any further deposition of anyone. Craig had explained that my attorney had merely made a flippant remark about the way my father tended to exaggerate the truth. The matter was behind me where, once again, I had to deal with another attack on Mr. Fisher.

The funny thing is that my mom has come to like my lawyer after all. They even socialize once in a while.

My grandpap passed away shortly following his diagnosis with cancer. This event was followed by a long list of unfortunate occurrences:

1) My stepmother, Jo-Ann, began to spiral into madness.

2) My federal civil lawsuit was dismissed against the security company, the McKeesport Police, School District, and Hose, among others.

3) I moved out on my own for good.

4) My therapist, Janice Pope, spent more time holding me back than helping me move forward with my mental health issues.

5) My relationship with the Spaicos soured unexpectedly.

In the midst of all this, I nonetheless grew stronger, and I found what I had feared I might never find in my life, what I had always been looking for: true love.

CLOSURE

As it turned out, the ordeal I faced in the years after my rescue from Hose was as challenging as what I faced during captivity. Still, I began to cope and thrive more progressively with each and every post-captivity hardship I faced. Some of the best examples of my growth in the wake of post-captivity hardships concern the way I handled Jo-Ann's mental-health meltdown, as well as the deterioration of my relationships with the Sparicos and Janice Pope. Mixed in with all of this, the loss of my federal civil lawsuit truly had a ripple effect on these relationships, as did my first romantic relationship since my ordeal with Hose.

In the end, the terrible mental breakdown Jo-Ann suffered served to help me accept and let go of the troubled relationship that had plagued me all the way back in 1995 and 1996.

It was the early summer of 2008. Jo-Ann was experiencing conflict with her siblings concerning her ailing mother, Dorcas. Ultimately, Jo-Ann became so delusional that she believed people were breaking into her home. Jo-Ann was calling the police to report intruders that did not exist. Through all of this, she began calling me to rant about her deranged beliefs. I would listen politely but soon realized that Jo-Ann was losing it mentally and that I would need to talk with my father about it. Just as he had been so many years ago with my mom, he was now faced with involuntarily committing Jo-Ann for psychiatric treatment. Eventually, Jo-Ann stabilized somewhat, and I successfully navigated this difficult situation.

I needed no reminding about the toll that mental illness takes on a family, but I felt able to help my father through it. Predictably, he did not seem to care for or appreciate my help. I was there for him, no matter what a jackass he had been at times before and since my release from Hose. "You only get one Mom and Dad," I was fond of reminding myself. Still, this mantra would only serve me so far, as the relationships with my father and Jo-Ann were about to become unsalvageable.

At this juncture, I also sought to put some distance between myself and the drama that went along with life in the home of my mother and Craig. As I was getting along better with Jo-Ann after Jo-Ann's mental meltdown, my mom and Craig became more and more irritable. This was the typical teeter-totter way in which they had reacted to the ups and downs in my relationships with my father and Jo-Ann. When I involved myself in my father's life, it always agitated my mother and Craig. To help get off of this roller coaster, I initially planned to move out into an efficiency apartment that was owned by Janice Pope, which she had recently renovated. Everything was all set, and Janice was going to allow me to live in the apartment at no charge; however, in September 2008, she completely changed her mind.

Coincidentally, at the same time, the federal judge presiding over my federal lawsuit against the McKeesport Police, School District, etcetera, threw the lawsuit out of court. In his opinion, Judge Gary L. Lancaster determined that my federal claims were barred by a legal concept known as the statute of limitations.

Statutes of limitation are laws that require legal claims to be brought within a certain period of time. Absurdly, Judge Lancaster maintained that the statute of limitation barred my legal claims because they had not been filed by October 14, 2001, while I was being held captive by Hose, notwithstanding the torture and threats to my life that I was enduring at that time. In essence, Judge Lancaster may have correctly noted that the acts and omissions by the various defendants giving rise to my federal claims all occurred back in 1995 and 1996, but he foolishly concluded that my claims accrued on my eighteenth birthday, once I was legally an adult, and that these claims remained viable for only two years thereafter, despite the fact that I was still held in captivity and tortured at that time. I appealed this decision.

Many people in my life, including Janice Pope, began to show real greed when it started to look unlikely that I would obtain financial gain anytime soon. This was especially true given the fact that my lawsuit had been dismissed. I now believe that Janice Pope ultimately wanted to profit off the proceeds of my lawsuit, and profit seemed a long way off, if coming at all, given the dismissal and appeal. Therefore, Janice decided to cut her losses and reneged on giving me the apartment. It was time for me to break away from her.

That Janice reneged on the apartment really had only part to do with my decision to seek out another therapist. More importantly, I had begun to feel as though I was getting better and healing mentally, while it simultaneously seemed to me that Janice was discouraging me from feeling better.

Furthermore, she had said some strange things to me in the past, such as insisting that I fire my lawyer. Janice continued to make comments to me that simply seemed out of bounds, including disapproval of a wonderful romantic relationship that was occurring in my life. Later, I would also learn that Janice Pope was actually related to a major figure in the St. Moritz security company that was a defendant in my lawsuit. So the apartment debacle was just part of many reasons why I broke ties with Janice, and it was for the better.

Likewise, my relationship with the Sparicos faltered at this same time, and just as with others, my romantic relationship and the loss of my lawsuit played a big part in the distance that opened up between the Sparicos and me in late 2008.

Joelle Sparico, in particular, reacted quite negatively to my evolving independence. I decided to take a job at K-Mart, and ultimately, to move out of my mom's home. I eventually fell in love with and moved in with a man I met while working at K-Mart. This bothered Joelle terribly.

Regardless, as I progressed in life further past my ordeal with Hose, I felt more capable of coping with everyday situations and thought it would be a good idea to try a job of some sort, really for the first time in my life. After all, I was approaching three years since that day in March 2006 when I escaped from Hose. I had come a long way in therapy and in my decision-making ability. I had taken a break from college and needed to occupy my time.

Thus, I began working in the customer service department at K-Mart in June of 2008. I worked there until December 2008. During this time, I met a man named Karl. That Karl was in his thirties, was separated from his wife, and had two teenage children bothered many in my life. My father and Jo-Ann immediately declared that they did not like Karl and wanted nothing to do with him. Joelle Sparico threatened me with the loss of her friendship if I continued to date Karl. This was the straw that broke the camel's back for me when it came to Joelle.

How dare she tell me how to live my life? Joelle and I had been through a great deal of the media circus together, but the relationship was never stable. Too often, Joelle had taken advantage or simply not been a good friend. After all, I ultimately gave Joelle the car I had received from a charity auction back in

2006, yet time and time again, Joelle would ignore my phone calls. Over and over again, Joelle would refuse to help me when I asked for and needed help. She had already meddled in my relationship with Joe Sparico by one time accusing me of " ... having the hots for my father." This sort of jealousy was preposterous. And Joelle was constantly pushing me, against the advice of Mr. Fisher, to "Go on Oprah."

Finally, I saw Joelle's true colors. She was only there for me when it suited her needs and interests. Once again, someone in my life was trying to control me, and I would be damned if Joelle was going to be the one. The end of our friendship came about via text message in early October 2008. It was Joelle who declared that, "Our friendship is over."

"Fine," I responded. "Have a nice life." Sadly, I have not spoken to her since. Such separation is sad for me, but I feel that I must recognize people for who they are and not for what I want them to be. I know that I must protect myself from ever being abused in any way or taken advantage of in any fashion or by anyone ever again.

This sort of strength on my part was the product of much therapy and treatment. I finally felt as if I was mentally stable and in control of my life. So, in November of 2008, I moved out on my own and into a home owned by Jo-Ann's mother, Dorcas, as Dorcas had moved in with Jo-Ann and my father. At this point, Karl and I were officially dating, but that did not, at first, prevent Jo-Ann from allowing me to rent Dorcas's home. All was well initially, but because my father and Jo-Ann did not like Karl, they began to cause trouble for us. As a result, I soon moved out of the house owned by Dorcas and into an apartment with Karl. This did not stop the madness with my father and Jo-Ann, a madness that would lead me to the inevitable conclusion that, just like with Joelle Sparico and Janice Pope, it was simply not healthy for me to have a relationship with them.

Shortly after I moved from the home owned by Dorcus and into a new place with Karl, Jo-Ann began to accuse me of petty thievery from Dorcas's home. These were the most ridiculous allegations ever, but that didn't stop Jo-Ann from marching up to my home, my father in tow, and forcing her way in to accost Karl and me. In the process, she even damaged the door to the home.

As usual, my father supported Jo-Ann in this mad attack against me. Even afterward, when Jo-Ann went on a McKeesport blog and began trashing me left and right, my father stood behind her. In the end, the whole situation dissolved to the point that my father began questioning once again all that I had suffered at the hands of Hose. In his most demeaning and unsupportive comments ever, he went so far as to tell me that he wanted to hear Hose's side of the story. That was the end for me. That was the moment I finally realized that my father had never been a father to me and never would be. It was liberating for me to tell this to him. We have not really spoken again since.

By contrast, my relationships with my mom and stepfather, Craig, have strengthened. They adore Karl, now my fiancé, and his children. They support me. They care. In spite of all that they have been through, my mom, Craig, and I have found a way to have a meaningful and positive relationship. Craig has been more of a father to me than Jerry Kach ever could or will be.

Furthermore, I have reconnected with many of my childhood friends through Facebook. I keep in touch with many of these friends, especially Ricky Ashcraft. Ricky is honorably discharged from the Navy and back in school to study nursing. It feels good to be in touch.

As the dismissal of my federal civil lawsuit was winding its way through the United States Court of Appeals for the Third Circuit, the Court of Appeals ordered a mediation to try and resolve the dispute. Miraculously and at long last, St. Moritz came to its senses and entered into a confidential settlement agreement with me. Finally, there was a measure of accountability from those, other than Hose and Sokol, who bore responsibility for my captivity. The McKeesport Police and School District defendants, however, refused to offer any sort of settlement, and the case wound up in front of a three-judge panel of the Third Circuit to review the dismissal of my federal civil lawsuit.

The Third Circuit praised Mr. Fisher as providing me with "…excellent representation." In the end, the Third Circuit demonstrated sympathy for me, concluding that I "suffered an indescribable ordeal that essentially stripped me of my adolescence and young adulthood."

But my "…unique circumstances notwithstanding, we are compelled to conclude that she forwent her right to relief in federal court by waiting too long to assert her rights."

Of course, I was profoundly disappointed by this decision; however, I accepted it. The opinion by the Third Circuit in my case was deemed "precedential," so my case will be forever preserved in the law. Others will be able to look back at it and see the way in which I fought for justice and the procedural impediments I faced. At best, I hope that people in power will read my case and realize that the Third Circuit determination sets a dangerous precedent that makes our schools less safe and our children more vulnerable to abuses of power by school employees and police by allowing those who abuse their power to do so without consequences. Indeed, if individuals and institutions of the state can get away with such recklessness and incompetence, there is no incentive to make it otherwise. Simply put, it is not fair that our schools and police are allowed to violate our rights without being held accountable, yet our system of justice allowed that to happen in my case. Maybe, hopefully, the law will change in response to this Third Circuit decision in my case so that justice and fairness are the same rather than distinct.

Regardless, as the Third Circuit decision in my case was reported just before Christmas 2009, I decided that I would not pursue any further legal review of my case. Instead, I was now free to say what I wanted about all that I had experienced, and I was no longer concerned that my words would be twisted and manipulated by the lawyers defending the McKeesport Police and School District. At last, as I was in the best spirits mentally and emotionally, my quest for justice had been rewarded, Hose and Sokol had been jailed, St. Moritz had accepted responsibility, and the McKeesport Police, as well as School District, could be exposed through this book. Nearly four years after I escaped the tyranny of Hose, I saw ahead of me a life filled with promise and possibility. My innocence may have been lost, but many would gain from that, I was certain.

Whatever those crotchety old judges said about my lawsuit, I made a difference merely by filing it. That's a good start in your 20's. At the same time, my mood soars now that I enjoy a normal relationship with Karl. I'm still in college seeking the education that I know will further my future. I've recently purchased a home with a mortgage in my name alone. Living life as an independent woman makes me proud.

And the garbage of my past has been recycled. Negative influences have been alleviated and positive influences nurtured. Even my health concerns inspire me to live my goals. Recovery is a process, not an event. I celebrate it all the same. Whatever awaits me, I'm optimistic. On top of everything I have suffered, remaining optimistic makes my life less ordinary, and provides me with the strength to overcome any hardship. Hardship is no excuse for a lack of fulfillment. Nothing in life is more than one person can handle. We are all blessed with the potential to overcome anything. It's not enough to survive, in light of it all, we must thrive.

For me, telling my story is part of thriving, but my life exceeds the memoir of a milk carton kid. All of the time my thoughts focus on creating a place for myself that, until now, I never imagined possible—on living my story that is still to come. Yet remembering the days of my childhood and the picnics I enjoyed in Monongahela, I try to recreate those good feelings and good times with my family and friends. I live with wholehearted appreciation for the great possibilities possessed by the potential I see in everything and everyone.

On the morning of Christmas 2009, I woke up to a beautiful sunrise and joy filled my heart. I had spent so many Christmases as a captive, held against my will. Yet, as I looked out my window into the sun high above me, I knew God is the one who kept me alive and finally released me to live.